LITTLE BOOK OF THE

ROYAL
AIR FORCE

LITTLE BOOK OF THE
ROYAL AIR FORCE

First published in the UK in 2011

© G2 Entertainment Limited 2011

www.G2ent.co.uk

Printed and bound in the EU

ISBN 978-1-907803-11-6

Contents

SSAFA Forces Help

The Soldiers, Sailors, Airmen and Families Association (SSAFA) Forces Help is the national charity supporting those who serve in our Armed Forces, those who used to serve, and the families of both. The qualifying period for assistance is just one day's service as well as close relatives.

SSAFA celebrated its 125th anniversary in 2010. The charity was founded in 1885 at the time that the Second Expeditionary Force set sail for operations in Egypt. Major James Gildea, an officer in the Royal Warwickshire Regiment, wrote a letter to the Times appealing for funds and volunteers to look after the families left behind.

In the 125 years that followed, SSAFA has made an unfailing commitment to the men and women of our Armed Forces. Through every war and conflict that Britain has fought in, the charity has been there to assist millions of different people.

Today, the scope and scale of SSAFA's work is enormous.
Last year, more than 50,000 people were helped by the charity.

New services continue to be established to provide vital practical support wherever and whenever it is needed. Recent examples include two SSAFA Norton Homes, enabling the families of wounded servicemen and women to be close to their loved ones when they need them most. New support groups have also been established for bereaved families and the families of our wounded.

These and several other types of assistance all have the common goal of ensuring that SSAFA remains the organisation that the Service Community and their families can depend on for support throughout their entire lives.

SSAFA|25
FIRST IN » LAST OUT

To find out more about the work of SSAFA
visit: **www.ssafa.org.uk** or call: **020 7403 8783**

Origins Of The
Royal Air Force

▼ Cartoon
dated circa1800.
Proposed use
of balloons to
raise Highland
Regiment troops
from where they
could fire at the
enemy as they
descended while
using their kilts
as parachutes.

Early Military Aviation

Throughout history, those who hold the high ground have gained a significant tactical advantage over their adversaries. From a lofty vantage point armies could be observed and their movements monitored, providing advance warning of attack. The high ground also provided a useful platform for firing weapons and observing their effect. However, the geography of battlefields often failed to provide the convenient high ground and as time passed, man became more resourceful in overcoming this.

Military aviation in Britain effectively began in 1878, with the formation by the Royal Engineers of a balloon unit first used in the 1880s during actions in the Sudan and in Bechuanaland, and again during the Boer War between 1899 and 1902. The Royal Engineers also used man-carrying kites during the early 1900s. These were gradually superseded by powered airships in 1907, and eventually by aeroplanes, with the formation of the first Royal Engineers Air Battalion in 1911. By 1912 there were only 11 qualified pilots, compared with over 260 pilots in the French Army Air Service.

▼ Cartoon dated circa1800. Proposed use of balloons to raise Highland Regiment troops from where they could fire at the enemy as they descended while using their kilts as parachutes.

The Royal Flying Corps

The Royal Flying Corps (RFC) was constituted by Royal Warrant on 13 April 1912, and took over the assets of the Royal Engineers Air Battalion on 13 May 1912. The RFC comprised a Military Wing, a Naval Wing, a Central Flying School (CFS), a Reserve force, and the Royal Aircraft Factory at Farnborough. The Military Wing comprised a Headquarters Unit, seven aeroplane squadrons, and one airship and man-carrying kite squadron.

The first recorded fatal aircraft accident occurred on 5 July 1912, near to Stonehenge in Wiltshire, when pilot Captain Eustace B Loraine and observer Staff-Sergeant R H V Wilson were killed. The order, "Flying will continue this evening as usual" was issued after this tragic event, thus beginning a tradition that has been maintained ever since.

The BE2 biplane was adopted as the main fighter aircraft for the RFC and, by the end of 1912, there were three squadrons each with twelve aircraft. A squadron of airships completed the inventory of powered flying machines.

At the commencement of hostilities in 1914 the RFC also used the Farman MF-7, the Avro 504, the Vickers FB5, the Bristol Scout, and the FE2. By May 1915, the RFC had around 166 aircraft – just over one-tenth of the strength of the French armed forces.

The first RFC casualties of World

▲ British troops crossing the Zand River during the Boer War campaign in 1900. An observation balloon keeps watch for enemy formations.

▶ Members of a Royal Flying Corps squadron on Salisbury Plain, Wiltshire, with a Royal Aircraft Factory B.E.2a aircraft, April 1913.

War I occurred in England on 12 August 1914. Lieutenant Robert R Skene – the first English pilot to perform a loop in an aeroplane – and Air Mechanic Ray Barlow lost their lives when their aircraft crashed en route to a rendezvous near Dover. Following the rendezvous, the RFC set off for France in a mass crossing of the English Channel with 60 machines.

The RFC's first action of the war was a two-aircraft reconnaissance mission on 19 August 1914. In order to save weight, each aircraft carried only a pilot instead of the usual crew of a pilot and an observer. This, coupled with poor weather, caused both pilots to lose their way and only one was able to complete his task. The RFC achieved its first victory on 25 August 1914 when Lieutenant C W Wilson and Lieutenant C E C Rabagliati took off in their Avro 504 and forced down a German Etrich Taube observation aircraft that had approached their aerodrome.

In April 1915, 2nd Lieutenant William Barnard Rhodes-Moorhouse became the first airman to be awarded the Victoria Cross. Although wounded whilst successfully completing a bombing raid on the rail junction at Kortrijk in Belgium, he brought his aircraft back to base and made his report before dying from his injuries the following day.

In August 1915, the appointment of Major-General Hugh Trenchard as RFC field commander signalled the change to a more aggressive approach to air warfare. Non-stop patrols over enemy lines led to heavy casualties and losses of aircraft. In July 1916, the RFC had a

◀ RFC metal and cloth badges.

Distinguished Flying Cross and Bar

Air Force Cross and Bar

Distinguished Flying Medal

Air Force Medal

total strength of 421 aircraft, equipping 27 squadrons, together with 14 balloons and four kite-balloon squadrons. At one point in 1916, an average of two RFC aircrew were lost every day, and by spring 1917 aircraft were being lost at the rate of almost 50 in a week.

Many losses were due to the superior aircraft and equipment of the opposing forces, but the lack of experienced

pilots and the inherent difficulty in controlling the effect of gyroscopic forces caused by the rotary engine, were contributing factors. The losses diminished considerably with the arrival of new fighter aircraft such as the Bristol Fighter, Sopwith Pup, Sopwith Camel, and SE5.

As personnel gained experience with their new equipment, the RFC's fortunes improved to such an extent that it had gained superiority over the German Air Force before the end of 1917. With the advent of the Airco DH-4 high-altitude, single-engine bomber, and the Handley Page heavy bomber that was capable of striking industrial targets within Germany, Trenchard was able to carry out the strategic bombing for which he was a strong advocate.

One of the more unusual types of mission undertaken by the RFC was the delivery of intelligence agents behind enemy lines. The first such mission took place on the morning of 13 September 1915, and ended in failure as the aircraft crashed. The pilot, Captain T W Mulcahy-Morgan, and his passenger were both badly injured, and were

▲ A Morane-Saulnier monoplane used by the R.F.C.(Royal Flying Corps), 1916.

◀ Major Lionel Wilmot Brabazon Rees VC, MC, of No. 32 Squadron, RFC. He rose to the rank of Group Captain before retiring from the RAF in 1931.

captured. However, two years later, the pilot escaped and returned to England. Later missions were more successful: in addition to delivering the agents, the RFC was also responsible for keeping them supplied with the carrier pigeons that were used to send their reports back to base. In 1916, a Special Duty Flight

was formed to handle these missions, together with other unusual assignments.

On 13 January 1917, Captain Clive Collett made the first British military parachute jump from a heavier-than-air craft. The jump, from an altitude of some 600 feet, was successful but the hierarchy in the RFC and the Air

ORIGINS OF THE ROYAL AIR FORCE

▶ Bristol Scout,
1916.

Board were opposed to the issuing of parachutes to pilots in case they were tempted to abandon the aircraft in an emergency instead of continuing the fight or bringing it back to base. The policy remained until 16 September 1918, when all single-seat aircraft were ordered to be fitted with parachutes.

Many pilots joined the RFC from their original regiments by first becoming observers. As there was no formal training for observers until 1917, many were sent on their first sortie with only a brief introduction to the aircraft from the pilot. Once certified as fully qualified, an observer was awarded the coveted half-wing 'O' brevet. Originally, the RFC observer was in command of the aircraft while the pilot simply flew the machine, but this was found to be less effective in combat than having the pilot in charge. Observers were usually given minimal flying training, sufficient only to land the aircraft if the pilot was killed or wounded. Experienced observers often volunteered or were selected for pilot training.

Eleven RFC members received the Victoria Cross during World War

I. Initially, the RFC was against the publicising of both victory totals and the exploits of their aircrews. However, due to immense interest from press and public, this policy was abandoned.

The Royal
Naval Air Service

In the early 1900s, the Royal Navy (RN) used balloons and airships for aerial reconnaissance. In 1911, the back of the naval airship *Mayfly* was broken in strong winds before it flew, leading the naval minister of the time, Winston Churchill, to call for the development of military aircraft.

In December 1911, the Royal

ORIGINS OF THE ROYAL AIR FORCE

▶ No. 1 Squadron pictured at Claremarais, France. Originally formed in 1878 as No. 1 Balloon Company, Royal Engineers, this squadron has been in continuous operation ever since 1912. Note the mascot beagle hound held by pilot (fourth from right).

Naval Flying School was formed. On the formation of the RFC in 1912, the Royal Navy was given the airships owned by the British Army and twelve aircraft for use in naval operations. The first flight from a moving ship took place in May 1912 and a year later the first seaplane carrier, *Hermes*, was commissioned. Around this time, the Royal Navy began to build a series of coastal air stations in support of its aviation operations.

The Royal Naval Air Service (RNAS) was formally established in January 1914 and, soon after, had a total of 217 pilots and 95 aircraft, of which 55 were seaplanes or flying boats, including the Curtiss H-16 flying boat. By the outbreak of war, the RNAS had more aircraft under its control than did the RFC.

The main roles of the RNAS were fleet reconnaissance, patrolling coasts for enemy ships and submarines, attacking enemy coastal territory, and defending Britain from enemy air raids. The RNAS also operated fighter squadrons equipped with the Bristol Scout, Sopwith Pup and Sopwith Camel aircraft on the Western Front.

▲ A Bristol fighter of No. 22 Squadron flies over Vert Galand aerodrome, France, on the inauguration day of the British Royal Air Force, 1st April 1918.

The leading air ace of the RNAS was Canadian-born Raymond Collishaw, with a total of 60 aircraft shot down, six of these in one day, and a further eight observation balloons destroyed.

The RNAS was severely criticised for its failure in preventing the Zeppelin bombing raids on mainland Britain and, in February 1916, the RFC was given responsibility for dealing with Zeppelins once they were over Britain. The RNAS then turned its efforts to the bombing of Zeppelins at their bases in Germany.

By the early part of 1918, the RNAS was able to muster over 67,000 personnel, almost 3,000 aircraft and more than 100 airships, along with 26 coastal stations. When absorbed into the new Royal Air Force, the RNAS squadrons were renumbered by the addition of 200 to their existing number and other units were allocated a squadron number in that '200' series.

The Royal Air Force

As the war progressed, problems with equipment supply, inter-service rivalry and the lack of a unified command structure became apparent. In July 1917, General Jan Smuts was appointed to report on these issues and recommended the amalgamation of the RFC and RNAS into a single organisation and command structure, headed by a new government ministry having equal standing with the War Office and the Admiralty. The new Air Ministry was tasked to plan for and oversee the amalgamation.

Initially many, including Sir Hugh Trenchard himself, felt that the new service would not provide the same level of support to the Army and Navy. Trenchard also had concerns about the long-term effects of combat fatigue on the pilots and aircrews. Under the RFC, pilots and observers were seconded from their regiments and could return there when they were unable to continue with their flying duties. This arrangement would not be available in the new amalgamated body.

The remit of the new Air Council, under Major-General Sir Hugh Trenchard, included the transfer of personnel, the creation of a rank and command structures, and the disciplinary arrangements for the new service. On 1 April 1918, the Royal Air Force (RAF) became the world's largest and the first truly independent air force. Also formed that year was a female branch of the new air force, the Women's Royal Air Force, as was the Royal Air Force Nursing Service.

At the time of the Armistice, the RAF had an inventory of 22,647 aircraft of all types, including 3,300 on its first-line strength, and 103 airships. These aircraft were operated by 133 squadrons and 15 flights overseas, and 55 squadrons in Britain. A further 75 squadrons were engaged in training. RAF units operated from 401 aerodromes at home and 274 overseas, with personnel totalling 27,333 officers and 263,837 other ranks.

Creation Of
The New Service

RAF Command Structure

Sir Hugh Trenchard, the 'Father of the RAF', was appointed Chief of the Air Staff in February 1919, a position he held until his retirement in 1929. He drafted the White Paper, commonly known as the Trenchard Memorandum, which outlined the proposed structure, organisation and development of the RAF.

The RAF's command structure has remained almost unchanged since its conception in 1919, although some of the functions and titles have since changed. The Air Ministry had political control over the RAF until 1964, when it passed to the Ministry of Defence. Overall control passed from the Air Council to the new Defence Council in 1964, and the Air Force Board is a committee of this.

Operational control has traditionally been delegated to 'commands'. The various commands have been formed on a functional or geographic basis, depending on prevailing military or political requirements. Since 1919, home commands have included Bomber, Fighter, Coastal, Transport, Signals, Balloon, Maintenance, Flying Training, and Technical Training Commands. Overseas commands date from those carried over from the RFC in 1918, and many more were created in Europe, the Middle East, Iraq, India, South East Asia and the Far East. Since the late 1960s, commands have been amalgamating until in 2007 a single HQ Air Command was formed from the merger of the two remaining commands.

Groups, Stations, Wings And Squadrons

Lower levels of operational control are delegated to 'Groups', which can control a number of 'Stations', each being headed by a station commander designated as Officer Commanding. A station can have a number of subordinate units based on it. Prior to World War II, RAF stations usually hosted a single 'squadron' or unit, and usually the head of the squadron or unit was also the station commander. Hostilities led to an increase in the number of units based at some stations and several stations were grouped together under the command of a Base Commander, usually with the rank of Air Commodore.

'Wings' are either sub-divisions of stations or can be an independent part of a group. Traditionally, a wing was a number of squadrons combining for operational purposes. Today's stations usually have three wings; Operations, Forward Support and Base Support, each of which may comprise a number of squadrons.

A squadron is a unit that in its

▶ RAF aeroplanes making their presence felt in Egypt with the roundel clearly visible, 1925.

operational flying role is comparable to an army regiment in that it can have traditions and a history, regardless of its present role or operational status, and can be awarded standards and battle honours. These are retained under the squadron number, even where the squadron's role is changed, until it is disbanded. Whenever such a squadron is reformed, it is entitled to display its predecessor squadron's battle honours and awards. Non-flying squadrons form a sub-division of a wing, and do not have the 'regimental' style of traditions or awards.

Squadrons are themselves sub-divided into 'flights', which may in turn be sub-divided into 'sections', according to their functional roles.

Branch Structure

On the formation of the RAF in 1918, officers were placed in one of eight branches of the service – Aeroplane and Seaplanes, Administrative, Airship, Kite Balloon, Medical, Observer, Staff Officer or Technical – according to the role they fulfilled. They could be transferred between branches depending upon the post they held.

After the war, Trenchard himself took the decision that all of his officers should be pilots, apart from in a very few specialised areas. The exceptions were in the Medical, Accountant, and Equipment Branches. All other officers would be qualified as pilots and placed in the General Duties (GD) Branch, where they would be responsible for all functional aspects of the RAF including flying, supervision of engineering, and carrying out staff and administrative duties.

This new, and smaller, branch structure remained virtually unchanged until the 1930s. Officers were first trained as pilots then, after a period on squadron duties, they could train in specialist engineering, armament and signals functions. They would then alternate these duties with those normally associated with a General Duties Officer, either in a flying post or as a staff officer. However, by 1940 the growing complexity of modern aircraft and equipment was beginning to demand a greater degree of specialisation than could be provided by such 'temporary' technical staff. As a result, it was decided to form a separate Technical Branch, with the sub-divisions of Engineering, Signals and Armament.

In 1939, air gunners were designate as official members of aircrew. Until then, air gunners had been recruited from the ground staff, and given extra pay for undertaking these duties: on cessation of flying duties, they reverted to their ground trades. The majority of air gunners were appointed to the rank of sergeant, but some were commissioned, to act as gunnery leaders. By the end of the war, some air gunners had actually risen to command squadrons. Air observers were also added in the new multiple-crew aircraft to relieve pilots of the additional tasks of navigation and bomb aiming.

The increased administrative demands of the enlarged wartime RAF were satisfied by the recruitment and appointment of retired officers, academics, and qualified administrators, who were commissioned into the new Administrative and Special Duties Branch.

The branch structure has undergone

several revisions to stand at 19 branches in 2010, ranging from Flying (Pilot), Operational Services (Aerospace Battle Management) and Engineering to Medical Support, Personnel (Training) and Chaplain Branch.

RAF Ranks

Prior to 27 August 1919, the RAF used rank titles of the British Army. From that date, a new rank structure was introduced based on rank titles from both the Army and the Royal Navy, together with some newly created designations.

Commissioned ranks within the Royal Navy were used as the basis for the ranks of Air Commodore, Group Captain, Wing Commander, Squadron Leader, and Flight Lieutenant. New ranks of Flying Officer and Pilot Officer were introduced at the lower end of the ladder. The more senior ranks, of Air Vice-Marshal and above, were also based on those of either navy or army origin. The commissioned rank structure in the RAF has remained virtually unchanged since 1919.

The non-commissioned officer (NCO) ranks, also created in 1919, were broadly those of the Army, except for the new rank of Flight Sergeant which took precedence over that of Sergeant. In the years that followed there were several changes in the rank structure for NCOs, abolishing the rank of Sergeant Major and later Warrant Officer Class 2, thus leaving Warrant Officer as the senior non-commissioned rank.

A new technician rank structure was introduced in 1951 whereby specific rank titles were given to personnel who had a technical or other specialisation, including aircraft engineering, and ground engineering tradesmen, bandsmen, and others. Ranks ranged from Junior Technician (no previous rank equivalent), Corporal Technician (equivalent to Corporal), Senior Technician (equivalent to Sergeant), Chief Technician (equivalent to Flight Sergeant), and Master Technician (equivalent to Warrant Officer).

Only two technician rank titles exist in the modern day RAF, those of Junior Technician and Chief Technician; the remaining technician levels are covered within the normal ranking structure.

The RAF Badge And Motto

The RAF badge was adopted at a meeting of the Air Council on 1 August 1918. It has been claimed that a tailor at the military tailors, Gieves Ltd, had designed the badge and that he originally drew an albatross, not an eagle. The design was similar to that of

▲ The Royal Air Force Badge. (© Crown Copyright)

the current badge except that the circlet surrounding the eagle was originally a garter and buckle. In December 1922 the design was formalised and submitted to the College of Arms for registration.

The origin of the motto of the RAF is believed to date back to the formation of the RFC in 1912. The commander of the RFC Military Wing, Colonel Frederick Sykes, tasked his officers to devise a motto for the new service

that would both inspire and encourage a strong *esprit de corps*. Anecdotally, Lieutenant J S Yule mentioned a phrase from Virgilian text: *sic itur ad astra* to a fellow junior officer. This, he developed into *per ardua ad astra*, which he translated as: "Through struggles to the stars".

It is also claimed that Yule had read the phrase in Sir Henry Rider Haggard's *The People of the Mist*, in which the following passage appears in Chapter 1: "To his right were two stately gates of iron fantastically wrought, supported by stone pillars on whose summit stood griffins of black marble embracing coats of arms and banners inscribed with the device Per Ardua ad Astra". Colonel Sykes gave his formal approval, and submitted it to the War Office. The King then approved its adoption for use in the RFC.

The RAF Roundel

During World War I, it became apparent that there was a need to identify aircraft in order to avoid confusion between enemy and friendly forces. In August 1914, orders were given for the Union Flag to be painted on the underside of the lower wings of all front line aircraft. Although satisfactory at lower levels,

only the cross was clearly visible at altitude, and was often mistaken for the German cross. It was then decided to adopt the French style of concentric circles, but with the red and blue rings transposed. A smaller version of the Union Flag was retained between the roundels and the wingtips, and a miniature Union Flag was painted on

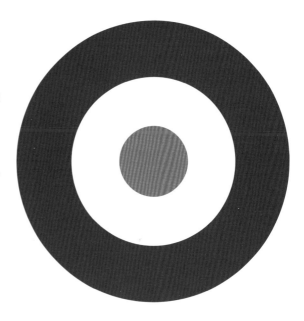

▲ The Royal Air Force roundel.

◄ The Royal Air Force flag being lowered for the last time at Station Headquarters RAF Gan, 1976.

▲▲ The White Ensign design that was rejected by the Admiralty.

▲ The Royal Air Force Ensign.

stripes formed the basis for RAF aircraft identifying markings for many years. The roundel has evolved along with the various aircraft camouflage and colour scheme changes through the years, in order to reflect the differing aircraft roles and/or their theatres of operations.

The RAF Ensign

There was a fair amount of inter-service wrangling and objection over the RAF Ensign. Many designs were considered, including some submitted by the general public. The final design employed the roundel of concentric red, white and blue circles that had been used on aircraft of both the RFC and RNAS, and the Union Flag in the top left-hand corner to show the mark of British authority. This design was accepted by the Admiralty, approved by the King, and introduced into service in December 1920.

the rudder. Aircraft of the Naval Wing of the RFC were marked with one red ring and the Union Flag.

In May 1915, the Union Flag on the aircraft rudder was replaced by red, white and blue vertical stripes and, in June of that year, the roundel was additionally painted on the upper surface of the wings. These roundels and

The RAF Ensign is flown daily at established RAF stations, being formally raised by duty personnel just before commencement of daily duties, and lowered at the end of the working day: it is also raised and lowered on specific occasions such as unit parades.

The Early Years

Early Overseas Operations

Before the formation of the RAF in 1918, British forces had already been engaged in aerial operations in Europe and the Middle East. Units of the RFC and RNAS had been involved in operations in Belgium and France, while there were others in Palestine, Egypt, Mesopotamia, Italy and India.

The Trenchard Memorandum stipulated the requirement for eight squadrons and a support depot in India, seven squadrons and a depot in Egypt, and a further three squadrons and a depot in Mesopotamia. These land-based aircraft were supplemented with three flights of seaplanes, one based in Malta, one in Alexandria in Egypt, and one on an aircraft carrier in the Mediterranean.

In May 1919, after the outbreak of the Third Afghan War, No 31 Squadron was involved in raids on the Afghan city of Jelalabad, with the loss of three aircraft. A bombing campaign by the RAF, in which leaflets giving warning of the impending action had been dropped on Afghan towns and villages to avoid civilian casualties, helped bring the war to an end in August 1919.

In 1922, a certain John Hume Ross enlisted in the RAF. Transferring to the

▼ Airmen aboard a train en-route for overseas posting.

▲ RAF personnel
embarking for
Mesopotamia,
1923.

Tank Corps in 1923 and changing his
name to Thomas Edward Shaw, the man
that was the famed 'Lawrence of Arabia'
eventually reverted to the RAF and
served thereafter as Aircraftsman
T E Shaw. First based in Karachi in
1927, he was later posted to Peshawar
and then to the town of Miranshah, near
to the Afghanistan border. Lawrence's
presence in the area was the subject of
many postulations, some believing that
his service in the RAF was a cover for
clandestine operations.

In 1932, in support of Iraqi troops
fighting against a small-scale revolt in
north-east Iraq, bombing raids were again
sometimes preceded by leaflet drops
warning of the forthcoming attacks, in an
attempt to minimise collateral casualties.
One of the earliest uses of aerial
broadcasts to ground forces occurred
when verbal warnings in Kurdish dialect
were given using a loudspeaker system
fitted to a Vickers Victoria transport
aircraft. The subsequent bombing raids
led to the surrender of the dissidents.

Air Control And Colonial Policing

Air Control was a policy advocated by Trenchard as a means of securing British interests overseas by suppressing uprisings from the air with fewer personnel and at lower cost. First used successfully against the 'Mad Mullah' and his supporters in Somaliland in 1920, where the vast expanses of territory made operations solely by ground troops difficult and time-consuming, it was not long before the Air Control policy was introduced elsewhere.

Trenchard proposed that the RAF be given full responsibility for conducting military operations in the former Ottoman provinces of Mesopotamia that forms part of modern Iraq. He asserted that the RAF could police the mandate with aircraft squadrons and some armoured-car squadrons, supported by a small number of British and locally-recruited troops, at a fraction of the cost of a large army garrison.

The financial benefit as well as the military strategy was readily accepted in Whitehall, and the proposal agreed. The RAF initially deployed a force

comprising eight squadrons of fighters and light bombers, including the DH9 reconnaissance/light bomber and the Vickers Vernon troop-transport/bomber. The Air Control policy worked to such effect that throughout the 1920s and 1930s the situation in Iraq was kept largely under control by bombing or sometimes by simply overflying the troublesome elements.

The effectiveness of Air Control was further emphasised in 1925, when Bristol Fighters and DH9s operated against Mahsud tribesmen on the Afghan border. Carrying out air operations including an air blockade

▼ Surplus SE5A fighters formed part of the Imperial Gift that led to the establishment of Commonwealth air forces.

and offensive actions against mountain strongholds, the campaign known as 'Pink's War', after Wing Commander R C M Pink who commanded the RAF units, was successfully concluded within two months with the loss of only one aircraft and its crew, and without the use of ground troops.

Policing of its territories, largely by the use of air power, became commonplace throughout the British Empire. Bombing raids replaced the traditional Army ground operations that had previously been mounted against dissidents on the Northwest Frontier in India, Aden and elsewhere.

Distance And Speed

In a time of post-war defence cuts, there had been lobbying by the War Office and the Admiralty, with support from some government ministers, who felt that the 'junior' service should revert to a lesser role under the two more senior armed services. Part of the RAF's opposition to the lobbying involved demonstrating the capabilities of its aircraft to travel over long distances at significantly higher speeds than surface transport could attain.

One of the most notable of the early long distance flying achievements was that of Major A MacLaren, who piloted a Handley Page V/1500 bomber from England to India, taking off on 13 December 1918 and reaching Delhi just over one month later. This particular aircraft subsequently took part in operations in Afghanistan, bombing Kabul on 24 May 1919.

On 14-15 June 1919, Captain John Alcock and Lieutenant Arthur Whitten Brown made the first non-stop flight across the Atlantic when they flew from St John's in Newfoundland to Clifden in County Galway, Ireland, in a modified Vickers Vimy bomber. Their total flight time was 16 hours 27 minutes, and ended in an ignominious crash landing in a boggy field. Both men were later knighted in recognition of their Trans-Atlantic achievement.

On 6 July the RAF airship R34 arrived in New York having departed

▲ Supermarine S6B.

from East Fortune in Scotland on 2 July, thus completing the first crossing of the Atlantic by an airship. Under the command of Major G H Scott, the R34 with its crew of 30 RAF and US Navy personnel, then commenced the return journey on 9 July, and landed at Pulham in Norfolk four days later.

In September 1927, the RAF took part in the Schneider Trophy competition in Venice in Italy, where a Supermarine S5 seaplane flown by Flight Lieutenant S N Webster won the race at an average speed of 281mph. The same aircraft set a closed circuit

THE EARLY YEARS

▶ The outright winners of the Schneider Trophy pictured in front of a Supermarine S6B, 1931.

record of 283mph over a distance of 100 kilometres. There was great opposition from within both the government and the Air Ministry before the RAF was permitted to defend of the Trophy in the 1929 race at Cowes on the Isle of Wight. This resulted in the Schneider Trophy being won for the second time by the RAF High Speed Flight, with a Supermarine S6 seaplane piloted by Flight Lieutenant H R D Waghorn at an average speed of 328mph. The engine for this aircraft had been privately funded by Rolls-Royce due to the reluctance of the Air Ministry to finance the building of "…a military engine with racing capabilities". R J Mitchell, who was later to design the Spitfire fighter, designed the S6 aircraft.

The period leading up to the 1931 Schneider Trophy races was full of political and military opposition to the continued involvement of the RAF. The government's view was that participation "… was not in accordance with the spirit of a sporting event …" which might "… not inconceivably lead to diplomatic incidents." The Air Ministry objected to the use of its pilots on the grounds that any publicity given to the team

would adversely affect morale within the Service. Even Sir Hugh Trenchard voiced his objections, saying that he could see "… nothing of value in it" as he believed that high-speed aircraft could be developed without the distraction and expense of the

Schneider Trophy competition.

Together with a donation of some £100,000 from Lady Lucy Houston, the widow of a wealthy shipping owner, British participation was ensured after the government relented. This second defence was successful and the race over the Solent was won by Flight Lieutenant J N Boothman in a Supermarine S6B seaplane powered by a 2,300hp Rolls-Royce R-Type engine at an average speed of 340.08mph, thus winning the Schneider Trophy outright.

Conflict On The Horizon

Countering The Threat

In July 1934, the Cabinet approved an increase in strength of the RAF to 111 front-line squadrons and 1,252 aircraft by 31 March 1939. This was considered to be sufficient to counter any foreseeable threat. Meanwhile, in Germany there was a continuing build-up of military strength leading to the formation of the Reichsluftwaffe in March 1935, in contravention of the terms of the Treaty of Versailles. Two months later, the title was abbreviated to become 'Luftwaffe'. In the same month, the British Government announced a further increase in the strength of the RAF to 1,500 aircraft, by 1937.

In 1936, a Balloon Barrage scheme was announced whereby balloon barrages would deter low-level attacks on important installations by forcing hostile aircraft to fly above the balloons, thus restricting the accuracy of hostile bombers and exposing them to anti-aircraft fire for longer periods. The RAF Volunteer Reserve (RAFVR) was also created with the intention of recruiting around 800 trainee pilots, 2,500 observers, and 3,200 wireless operator/air gunners between 1936 and 1938. These target numbers were increased as the international situation deteriorated.

A series of air defence exercises were held to test the country's defences the same year. For the exercises it was assumed, correctly as was later proved, that enemy forces would enter British airspace over the coast of south-east England. It provided a test of the effectiveness of the Observer Corps, which had passed to Air Ministry control in order to

provide closer collaboration with the air defence organisation.

The air exercises demonstrably illustrated the ineffectiveness of both the defensive equipment and the procedures in use in providing advance warning of enemy air attack at the time. More than half of the bombers reached their exercise targets unopposed and in many cases undetected, even though their routes and targets were known in advance.

The Air Ministry set out to rectify the situation by involving Robert Watson-Watt, Superintendent of the

▲ Royal Air Force Westland Wapiti aircraft flying over rugged landscape of Iraq, 1934.

Radio Research Station at Slough. It had been discovered that the radio energy that was reflected from an aircraft could be detected at 'useful' ranges. To demonstrate the viability of the theory, Watson-Watt and his team used powerful short wave transmissions from the BBC transmitter station at Daventry, and measured the signals reflected from a RAF Heyford bomber. Detection ranges of up to eight miles were achieved, leading to further funding and, within a few months, ranges of 40 miles were being reliably achieved. By August 1936, the first station was in operation at Bawdsey in Suffolk and a further four, located in a chain around the coast, shortly afterwards.

Plots of incoming aircraft were passed by telephone to a central operations room, where the information could be co-ordinated with visual sighting reports received from the Royal Observer Corps and data from the radio direction-finding system. Using the combined data, RAF personnel based at Biggin Hill in Kent developed fighter control and interception techniques that were considered to be effective for daytime use against larger groups of aircraft, but not against smaller, dispersed groups at night. This led to experiments to test airborne versions of the system.

Initial tests detected a Heyford bomber at a range of over ten miles. The airborne system proved effective in poor weather condition and against surface ships at several miles' range. These initial trials led to the further development of Air Interception (AI) and Air to Surface Vessel (ASV) equipment, and the construction of Chain Home Low (CHL) stations around the coasts of Britain to detect low-flying intruders. All of these developments were to prove vital to the defence of the country in the coming years.

Reacting to the Munich crisis in 1938, the RAF introduced emergency measures in preparation for war, including the establishment of Mobilisation Pools for the purpose of organising large groups of personnel and their subsequent movement drafts.

The early months of 1939 saw the formation of the Auxiliary Air Force Reserve. This was created to enable ex-members of the Auxiliary Air Force to serve with auxiliary flying squadrons in an emergency. The women's services were also augmented with the establishment of the Women's Auxiliary Air Force.

◀ RAF Air Pageant in 1930 at Hendon Aerodrome, now the site of the Royal Air Force Museum.

In June 1939, as the political situation in Europe continued to worsen, the Secretary of State for Air, Sir Kingsley Wood, announced that the RAF would impress civil aircraft into service in the event of war. During the summer, Bomber Command took part in a series of navigational exercises over Central and Southern France involving around 240 aircraft for both 'training' and 'show of strength' purposes. Further exercises took place, culminating in a final 'practice' in which over 1,300 aircraft participated.

The End Of The Biplane Era

In the 1930s the biplane continued to form the mainstay of RAF front-line aircraft. Included in this category was a varied assortment of flying machines, some pleasing to the eye, others less than attractive to the purist. Falling into the latter classification were aircraft such as the Handley Page Hinaidi twin-engine bomber that was in operational service between 1929 and 1933. Some were converted to troop transport aircraft and used extensively throughout the Middle East.

The most numerous fighter aircraft of the RAF in the early 1930s was the Bristol Bulldog that had entered service in 1929. This biplane fighter was fitted with a Bristol Jupiter engine and was capable of speeds of almost 180mph, with a range of some 300 miles. Armed with two 0.303in machine guns, it could also carry four 20lb bombs. Apart from being an excellent aeroplane, one of its main attributes was that it was relatively economical to operate and maintain – an important feature in times of constrained defence budgets.

▲ Hawker Hart light bomber circa 1930.

Among the more aesthetically pleasing aircraft types of the biplane era were those produced by the Hawker Company. The Hawker military biplanes were evolutions of the Sopwith aircraft of World War I. In the late 1920s, following the introduction of the Rolls-Royce V12 'F-series' engine and the development of metal airframe structures, the Hawker Company produced the sleek and beautiful Fury fighter, and the Hart two-seater light-bomber and training aircraft. The Fury was a direct predecessor of the Hurricane; the Hart led to many

▲ Bristol Bulldog planes being constructed at Filton.

▶ Juan de la Cierva in the cockpit of his autogiro, November 1933.

variants, including the Hind and the Audax that were in service until the outbreak of World War II. The Hart was a particularly good aircraft, with a rapid rate of climb, and was excellent in aerobatics. Although a bomber, in 1930

it could outpace every fighter of its day.

In August 1934, the first of a batch of twelve Avro Rota Mark I autogiros entered service with the School of Army Co-operation at RAF Old Sarum in Wiltshire, becoming the first rotary-wing aircraft to be operated by the RAF. Designated the Cierva C30A, the autogiro had been designed and developed by the Spaniard, Juan de la Cierva, who had moved to Britain in the mid-1920s and sold licenses for production in several countries including France, Britain and Germany. The main feature of this aircraft was that the rotor, which auto-rotated freely in normal flight, could also be spun-up before takeoff, thus decreasing the distance required for the autogiro to become airborne to around 90ft. Although not capable of hovering, the Rota could fly very slowly and, with a landing speed of around 10mph, was considered to be relatively easy to fly compared to its successor, the helicopter. The aircraft remained in service with the RAF in a variety of roles, including radar calibration duties, until 1945.

During 1935 and 1936, several new aircraft types entered service, including the Boulton Paul Overstrand. This was the last twin-engine biplane bomber to fly with the service and the first to be equipped with an enclosed, power-operated gun turret.

▲ Hawker Hurricanes under construction, 1938.

Other notable debutantes of the period were the Gloster Gauntlet, Hawker Fury II, Hawker Hind and the Short Singapore III flying boat.

The Rise Of The Monoplane

The Avro Anson monoplane, designed for coastal reconnaissance, was the first aircraft in RAF service to have a retractable undercarriage. Although advanced for the mid-1930s, rapid improvements in aircraft performance meant that the Anson was hopelessly outclassed by the outbreak of war in 1939.

When it entered service in December 1937, the Hawker Hurricane became the first monoplane fighter aircraft to be adopted by the RAF, and the first combat aircraft operated by the service that was capable of exceeding 300mph in level flight. It was the first fighter with a retractable undercarriage, and the first to be armed with eight guns.

Designed by Sidney Camm, the Hurricane was based on the Hawker Fury biplane fighter but re-designed around the new Rolls-Royce Merlin engine. The Hurricane was a traditional Hawker design with a tubular metal

fuselage frame constructed with
mechanically fastened joints rather
than being welded. The fuselage was
covered with a fabric, similar to that of
its predecessor the Fury. Each wing was
constructed with two steel spars and
ribs, and was also fabric covered. From
1939, the wing surfaces were skinned
with sheet metal.

R J Mitchell, chief designer at
Supermarine, had been responsible for
the design of the successful Schneider
Trophy-winning seaplanes in the late
1920s and early 1930s. In 1933 the RAF
turned down his first fighter design, the
Type 224, as being unsuitable for use as

an interceptor fighter. This led to Mitchell
designing a revolutionary new airframe
around the Rolls-Royce PV12 engine
that later became the Merlin engine.

The new aircraft, designated F37/34,
showed great potential even while still a
'paper aeroplane' on the drawing board.
Its maiden flight on 5 March 1936
at Eastleigh near Southampton was
more than satisfactory, even though the
undercarriage was locked down and no
armament had been fitted. With a design
calculation for a top speed of 350mph,
it actually reached 349mph during trials.
Together with its high speed, excellent
handling and eight-gun armament, the

Spitfire was destined to go down in history as one of the greatest fighter aircraft of its era, as well as being one of great aesthetic appeal.

The forerunner of the aircraft that was to become the backbone of the RAF bomber force in the first two years of World War II was originally known as the Crecy and first flew in 1936. The Vickers Wellington, as it was eventually named, was popularly known as 'the Wimpy' by service personnel, after J Wellington Wimpy, a character from the Popeye cartoons. The Wellington used a unique geodetic construction design similar to that used by Barnes Wallis for airships and also used by Vickers in the single-engine Wellesley bomber. This type of construction was extremely strong and relatively light and easy to repair, but took longer to construct than the monocoque system used in other aircraft. The Wellington MkI was powered by two 1,050hp Bristol Pegasus engines, and equipped with two power-operated gun turrets. It could carry a bomb load of around 4,500lb. The MkI version first entered service in October 1938 and was to

outlast its more numerous counterparts, the twin-engine Handley Page Hampden and Armstrong Whitworth Whitley bombers, in operational use.

The Jet Engine

Frank Whittle applied to join the RAF as an apprentice at the age of 16 in January 1923. He was initially rejected on the grounds of his small stature, but following an intensive fitness programme he re-applied six months later and was accepted. While at the Royal Air Force College at Cranwell in Lincolnshire, he wrote a thesis exploring the possibilities of flight at higher altitudes and speeds than could be achieved by contemporary aircraft. He expounded the potential of both rocket propulsion and the gas turbine – the latter possibly to be used to drive a ducted propeller or fan. The concept of pure jet propulsion was not formulated until the year after he left Cranwell. The Air Ministry was not impressed, believing that the gas turbine was impracticable, but undeterred, Whittle took out a patent in 1930. He later attended the Officers' School of Engineering at Henlow in Bedfordshire

▲ Gloster Meteor.

where, in 1934, he graduated with exceptional results. This led to him entering Cambridge University, as an undergraduate in Mechanical Sciences.

With support from friends who had arranged financial backing from a London bank, Whittle began construction of his first engine in 1935. This engine was first run in April 1937 and although it was simply a test rig, it successfully demonstrated the feasibility of the turbo-jet concept. After negotiations with a more receptive Air Ministry, as he was still a serving officer, Power Jets Ltd was formed and Whittle was allotted shares in return for assigning all his patent rights to the company. A contract for the design of an experimental bench engine, the 'WU', was awarded to the British Thomson

ORIGINS OF THE ROYAL AIR FORCE

▶ Rear view of a Meteor Mark IV, which was used in an attempt to raise the world's air speed record in 1946.

Houston Company at Rugby. After gaining his first class honours degree at Cambridge, Whittle was granted a further post-graduate year to supervise the work on the WU engine, which made its first run on 12 April 1937.

Whittle was appointed to the Special Duty List and continued to work for Power Jets as Honorary Chief Engineer. By June 1939, the work had progressed sufficiently for the Air Ministry to place an order for a flight engine, the W1, with the company. The Gloster Aircraft Company was contracted to build an experimental aircraft, the E28/39, powered by the W1. The highly successful first test flights on 15 May 1941 resulted in an expansion of the project, and the beginning of co-operation between Britain and the USA on the development of the turbo-jet engine. Even before the outcome of the test flights, a decision was taken to build a twin-engine fighter, the Gloster F9/40 (Meteor), using the more powerful W2B engine. In 1944, the Meteor entered service and was the only Allied jet to be operational in World War ll.

Their Finest Hour

Operations Commence

▶ Loading propaganda leaflets onto a Whitley bomber in early 1940.

In January 1939, the RAF operational aircraft inventory consisted of 135 squadrons: 74 bomber, 27 fighter, 12 army co-operation, 17 reconnaissance, 4 torpedo-bomber and 1 communications squadron. At the same time, the strength of the Auxiliary Air Force totalled 19 squadrons: 3 bomber, 11 fighter, 2 army co-operation and 3 reconnaissance squadrons.

On the day that war was declared, a Bristol Blenheim IV aircraft became the first RAF aircraft to enter German airspace, carrying out a visual and photographic reconnaissance of German naval ports and shipping.

The RAF's first offensive sorties also took place on 3 September 1939, when 18 Handley Page Hampdens and 9 Vickers Wellingtons of Bomber Command took part in an operation against German naval shipping. On this occasion, they failed to locate any targets and returned to base. This first day of war saw the first RAF casualty when Pilot Officer John Noel Isaac of No 600 Squadron became the first British serviceman to die in the war. His Bristol Blenheim crashed into Heading Street in Hendon less than two hours after the declaration of war.

On the same night, seven Whitley bombers of No 58 Squadron and three from No 51 Squadron dropped propaganda leaflets over Germany. Nearly six million copies of the leaflet carrying a message headed "Warning! A Message from Britain" were dropped over Bremen, Hamburg and the Ruhr. The following night a further three million leaflets were dropped and during the first month of the war more than twenty million leaflets, with five different messages, were discharged over enemy territory.

The war was to last only one day for Sergeant George Booth, an observer with No 107 Squadron. On

4 September his Blenheim aircraft was shot down over the German coast and he was captured, thereby earning the dubious distinction of becoming the first member of the RAF to become a prisoner of war. This same day also saw

a concerted bomber attack on German warships at Wilhelmshafen, Brunsbüttel and the Schillig Roads. Fourteen Wellingtons and 15 Bristol Blenheims took part in the raid. Ten Blenheims attacked the pocket battleship *Admiral Scheer* at Wilhelmshafen and scored three hits, but the bombs failed to detonate. In the same port, there was a bizarre coincidence when a Blenheim piloted by Flying Officer H L Emden attacked a cruiser with the same name and crashed onto the *Emden*'s deck, killing all four crew. Seventeen aircrew failed to return from this mission.

After the first raids by the Luftwaffe over Britain on 6 September, a technical fault at the 'Chain Home' radar direction-finding station at Canewdon in Essex, together with errors made within the Fighter Command control system, resulted in friendly aircraft being incorrectly identified as an incoming air raid. Hurricane fighters from No 56 Squadron at North Weald in Essex 'scrambled' to intercept the supposed raiders were also identified as hostile. Further squadrons were then scrambled and, amid the confusion, a section of Spitfires from No 74 Squadron at

Hornchurch mistakenly identified two of the Hurricanes as Messerschmitt Bf109s and shot them down, killing one of the pilots. This series of events became known as 'The Battle of Barking Creek', and led to a sweeping review of Fighter Command's plotting systems and operational procedures.

As a result, an Identification Friend or Foe (IFF) system was fitted in RAF aircraft, thus enabling radar operators to differentiate between the radar signal returns of enemy and friendly aircraft. Initially, the system relied on the 'passive' reflection of radar signals by target aircraft, but an 'active' system that utilised a transponder mounted in the aircraft was being developed in early 1939. The principle remains in use today, in both military and civil aviation.

Later in September, a Dornier Do 18 flying boat became the first enemy aircraft to be shot down during operations against Britain, the success being credited to a Blackburn Skua of No 803 Squadron Fleet Air Arm from HMS *Ark Royal*. The first RAF victory, and the first by an aircraft operating from a British land base, took place on 8 October 1939. An American-built

◀ Bristol Blenheim IV light bomber, circa 1940.

Lockheed Hudson of No 224 Squadron shot down another Dornier Do 18 flying boat to achieve this milestone victory.

Britain's flying boats were generally used for long-range anti-submarine and shipping patrols. Developed from the Short Brothers' range of civil aircraft, the Sunderland was a particularly useful aircraft in this role. With an endurance of around 20 hours, the Sunderland was a significant improvement on the earlier biplane flying boats. With self-defence armament that earned it the German nickname of 'flying porcupine', it frequently beat off attacks by numbers of enemy aircraft, including one occasion when a Sunderland shot down three out of a group of six Junkers Ju 88s, and caused the remaining three to disengage.

Although the Sunderland was a true 'boat', in that it required a beaching trolley to move it onto dry land, the American-built Consolidated Catalina was an amphibian, with retractable wing tip floats and undercarriage. The Catalina was a classic aircraft of its time: more than 600 were acquired by the RAF, and served with distinction throughout World War II.

The Battle
Of Britain

The appointment of Winston Churchill
as Prime Minister in 1940 seemed
to give Britain a new-found strength
against adversity. Churchill was
renowned for his rousing, if somewhat
theatrical, speeches and the RAF in
particular was on the receiving end
of some of his most impassioned
oratory. During the summer of 1940,
he said, "The Navy can lose us the
war, but only the Air Force can win it.
Therefore our supreme effort must be
to gain overwhelming mastery in the
air. The Fighters are our salvation, but
the Bombers alone provide the means
of victory."

At the start of the war, Germany
had around 4,000 aircraft compared to
Britain's front-line strength of 1,660.
After the fall of France, the Luftwaffe
had almost 3,000 aircraft based in the
near continent including 1,400 bombers,
300 dive bombers, 800 single-engine
fighters and 240 twin-engine fighter
bombers. The RAF total included
around 800 Hurricanes and Spitfires, of
which about 660 were serviceable in

mid-1940. Production of new aircraft
was increasing rapidly, but a major
problem was the shortage of trained
crews to fly them, not least the skilled
fighter pilots necessary for air defence
duties. In April 1940, the Empire Air
Training Scheme (later renamed the
British Commonwealth Air Training
Plan) was introduced in order to bolster
the number of aircrew.

As a necessary preliminary to
the invasion of Britain, code-named
Operation Sealion, the Germans
needed control of the Channel ports
to prevent Royal Navy forces attacking
the invasion fleet on its way to the
beaches of Kent and Sussex. For this,
the Germans also needed to control the
air. Although it possessed large numbers
of bombers, the Luftwaffe's fighters had
insufficient range to give the bombers
adequate air cover for much of their
time over British territory. With the
benefit of radar and the visual sightings
of enemy aircraft by the Observer Corps
from their posts in Kent and around
the Thames estuary, fighter controllers
were able to plot the positions of enemy
aircraft while they were over the south-
east corner of England.

◀ Pilots
scramble to
their Hurricane
fighters, 1939.

▲ Boulton Paul Defiant fighter, 1940.

▶ The Spitfire and the Hurricane, defenders of the Realm.

The main phase of the battle began on 10 July 1940. By the end of that month, RAF losses were around 150 aircraft, while the Luftwaffe had lost almost 270. In August, the Germans began to attack the airfields of Fighter Command, together with its operations rooms and radar stations, in an attempt to destroy the RAF on the ground. By this time most of the Stuka dive bombers had been destroyed, thus reducing the Luftwaffe's ability to carry out sufficiently accurate bombing attacks on the British radar stations to take them out of operation. A period of

bad weather also hampered the German effort. Even so, their attacks on RAF airfields put six of the seven main fighter bases out of action in the two weeks following 23 August, almost destroying Biggin Hill entirely. However, German losses were mounting: during this offensive they lost around 1,000 aircraft, while the RAF lost 550.

Around this time, the Germans made a series of strategic and tactical errors. Goering, the Luftwaffe commander, ordered the bombing of British radar installations to cease in the mistaken belief that the stations were of little

▲ Fairey Battle lightbomber being loaded with 250lb general purpose bombs, 1940.

importance. The Germans also turned their bombing attacks toward Britain's cities in an attempt to demoralise the civilian population into surrender. These changes in policy proved to be decisive factors in the battle.

The last major air engagement in this phase of the war took place on 15 September 1940, a date remembered by the RAF as 'Battle of Britain Day'.

On that day 60 Luftwaffe aircraft were destroyed at a cost of 28 RAF aircraft. On 17 September Hitler postponed indefinitely the invasion of Britain and turned his attentions towards Russia, although his 'Blitzkrieg' bombing attacks against Britain's towns and cities continued.

Propaganda claims and counter-claims were rife; at one point the Germans claimed the destruction of over 3,000 RAF aircraft – more than its entire strength – the actual tally being around 650. In turn, the British government claimed that the RAF had shot down 2,698 German aircraft, whereas this figure should have been around 1,100.

After the battle, Winston Churchill made another of his memorable speeches, in which he said: "Never in the field of human conflict was so much owed by so many to so few."

▲ Ground crew reloading a Hurricane fighter's machine guns during the Battle of Britain.

Bombs Gone!

In the early months of the war, RAF bombers based in Britain were used mainly against enemy shipping, often in their ports or at their anchorages off the German coast. On 10 May 1940, in the first major attack on German land targets, eight Whitley bombers from Nos 77 and 102 Squadrons raided communications sites located inland to the west of the Rhine. The strategic air offensive against targets within Germany began on 15 May 1940, when a Bomber Command force of 99 aircraft struck at 16 separate targets in the Ruhr area. Although no aircraft were lost to enemy action, a Vickers Wellington from No 115 Squadron crashed into high ground near Rouen in France, killing its crew of five.

Before the retreat from continental Europe, ten squadrons of Fairey Battle light bombers of the Advanced Air Striking Force (AASF) operated there in support of ground troops. On 20 September 1940 the first aerial engagement between the RAF and the Luftwaffe took place near Saarbrücken, when three Messerschmitt Bf109s attacked three Fairey Battles of No 88 Squadron,

AASF. Two of the Battles were shot down.

The first long-range bombing raid of the war took place on the night of 11 June 1940 when a force of 36 Armstrong Whitworth Whitley aircraft set out from Britain for targets in Italy. Stopping to refuel in the Channel Islands, they were hampered by bad weather. As a consequence, only 13 made their attacks on the Italian cities of Genoa and Turin. Two aircraft failed to return.

Three days later, aircraft from the Bomber Command unit known as 'Haddock Force', based in the south of France, mounted their first operation against an Italian target. However, due to particularly bad weather only one of the Vickers Wellingtons was able to attack the target at Genoa. Haddock Force was disbanded shortly afterwards, mainly because of objections from the local government, who ordered the blocking of runways by French soldiers to prevent bombers from taking off on missions that might lead to reprisals against the local population by the German forces.

During the period of the Battle of Britain, the RAF continued to carry out bombing raids over enemy occupied territories. Blenheim bombers

frequently targeted the German invasion fleet that was gathering in the Channel ports of France. These aircraft were also used against military installations and airfields in Norway and strategic targets in Germany. The 'intruder' attacks against airfields were carried out in daylight, and resulted in heavy losses of valuable aircraft and crews. One such attack on 9 July 1940, against the Norwegian airfield at Stavanger, resulted in the loss of seven of the twelve aircraft involved. A day later, No 107 Squadron lost five out of the six Blenheims that raided the French city of Amiens.

Strategic targets in Germany received the attention of Bomber Command throughout the war. The canals and

waterways of the German transport system were bombed on a regular basis, especially the lock gates, bridges and aqueducts. The main targets were the Dortmund-Ems and Mittelland Canals, and the Munster Aqueduct, which were heavily defended by anti-aircraft batteries, resulting in heavy losses of RAF aircraft. Attacks using relatively small groups of less than 20 Hampden bombers were carried out until late September 1940. They were resumed in September 1943 by Lancasters and Mosquitoes, and continued until March 1945. Much larger numbers of bombers, sometimes over 200, carried out these raids with their targets being identified and marked by the Mosquitoes of the Pathfinder force. The raids culminated in the destruction of the Bielefeld Viaduct on 14 March 1945, when a Lancaster of No 617 Squadron dropped a 22,000lb bomb, the 'Grand Slam', with devastating effect.

The Thousand Bomber Raids

A series of 'thousand bomber' raids took place between the end of May and mid-August 1942. The concept of attempting to force the enemy into submission by attacking largely civilian targets was the idea of Commander-in-Chief of Bomber Command Sir

Arthur Harris, and was not popular among his contemporaries. Using an eclectic assortment of aircraft and crews, including instructors and crews that were in the later stages of their training, Harris achieved a total of 1,047 bombers.

The first raid was planned for Hamburg but, due to bad visibility over the target, the first target became Cologne. Major damage to factories, infrastructure and housing ensued, resulting in a quarter of the population fleeing the city. Bomber Command lost 41 aircraft on that one night.

The thousand-bomber raids were mainly successful. Losses through collision between the close formation aircraft were relatively few, the morale of Bomber Command personnel improved as its future was assured, and the effect on the enemy was devastating. The raids also served to elevate the stature of 'Bomber' Harris in the public eye. Although the raids were restricted mainly to targets nearer the coast during the short summer nights, other targets still received visits from Lancasters and other British aircraft. Not all were successful in their missions, notably those carrying out attacks against Essen and Duisburg. However, the bomber raids over Germany, in which large numbers of aircraft were used, continued. On 21 June 1943, a total of 705 bombers attacked Krefeld and virtually destroyed the city, with the loss of 44 aircraft mainly to attack by night fighters. At the end of July and beginning of August, further large-scale raids took place on Hamburg by 777 aircraft and Nuremburg by 740 aircraft. These totals also include aircraft from the 8th United States Army Air Force (USAAF), which participated in large numbers using B-17 Flying Fortresses.

◀ Avro Lancaster of the Battle of Britain Memorial Flight.

The Dambusters

Formed on 21 March 1943 under the command of Wing Commander Guy Gibson, No 617 Squadron was staffed by crews specially selected for the particular nature of the missions it was to undertake. Their targets were the Mohne and Eder Dams in the Ruhr valley. After six weeks' intensive training, 19 Lancasters were dispatched in three waves, each aircraft armed with a 'bouncing' bomb developed by Barnes Wallis for the specific purpose of attacking and destroying the German dams. The entire operation was carried out at low level to escape attack from German night fighters, and the bombs had to be released at a specific height, just above the surface of the water behind the dams.

Only twelve of the Lancasters made it to the target area. Wing Commander Gibson's aircraft and four others bombed the Mohne Dam and breached it, in spite of intense fire from the defending flak guns. Three aircraft went on to breach the Eder Dam, while two others unsuccessfully attacked the Sorpe Dam, as did a single aircraft against the Schwelme Dam. The twelfth aircraft failed to find its target. Three aircraft were shot down after they had completed their bombing run. For this raid, which caused widespread damage and flooding in the Ruhr valley, and also for a series of other exceptionally courageous missions, Gibson was later awarded the Victoria Cross. Of his comrades, 34 received decorations.

Peenemunde

A major bomber offensive on the night of 17–18 August 1943, code-named Operation Hydra, involving 596 aircraft from Bomber Command targeted Peenemunde, the main experimental establishment where the V-1 flying bomb and the V-2 rocket were developed and tested. A diversionary raid on Berlin, code-named Operation Whitebait, was made by a force of Mosquitoes. The main stream of bombers en route to Peenemunde met with little opposition from night fighters, the raid being made on a reciprocal heading from that expected by the Germans as the initial course of the bomber stream was in a direction that indicated a possible attack in the area of Berlin. This belief was made credible by the diversionary raid carried out by the Mosquitoes. After overflying the Jutland peninsula, the bombers turned to make their bombing runs from a south-easterly direction.

The raid was the largest carried out by Bomber Command in the second half of the war, against such a small objective, and was also the first in which a 'Master Bomber' directed operations over the target. The attack was considered successful in that it delayed the development of the V-2 by several months, thereby reducing the overall effectiveness of the German rocket attacks. Unfortunately, the attack also resulted in the deaths of several hundred foreign workers, mostly Polish, as some bombs fell on

◄ Bristol Beaufort, circa 1943.

a workers' camp. Bomber Command lost 23 Lancasters, 15 Halifaxes, and 2 Stirlings, most of these falling victim to the late-arriving Messerschmitt Me-110 night fighters. Two of the fighters, equipped with twin 'Schrage Musik' upward firing 20mm cannon armament, shot down at least six of the bombers as they attacked the homeward-bound aircraft stream.

Dresden

One of the most controversial and devastating attacks carried out on a single target was the bombing of Dresden in February 1945. This raid was part of the Combined Bomber Offensive, in which night attacks were carried out by the RAF, followed the next day by raids from 8th USAAF bombers. The political justification for this offensive was to assist the Russian advance from the east and hindering German communications and troop movements. The intention was to create firestorms by dropping large quantities of incendiary bombs over a specific target, thus causing the extremely hot air to rise rapidly and draw colder air to the centre of the conflagration. The intense

heat and strong winds would cause considerable damage to both life and property in the target area.

Dresden was considered to be a good target, being relatively lightly defended by anti-aircraft batteries. Alternative targets were designated at Chemnitz and Leipzig: all were located behind the German front, close to the line of battle as the Russians advanced westward, and all were major communications centres crucial to the German war plan.

On 13 February 1945, the RAF sent 773 Lancasters to bomb Dresden. This was followed over the next two days by more than 500 bombers from the USAAF, resulting in the near-destruction of a city with a population of more than 650,000, and causing many thousands of refugees to flee the Russian advance.

As the war drew towards its inevitable end, there was a more humanitarian motive to the flights carried out by some aircraft of Bomber Command. In Operation Manna, RAF bombers took part in mass food drops to the Dutch population in areas that were still occupied by German forces. Between 29 April and 8 May 1945, approximately 6,685 tons of food were delivered by the

RAF, together with a further 3,700 tons dropped by the 8th USAAF.

First Jet Operations

The first operational jet fighter squadron in the RAF was No 616 Squadron, a detached flight of seven Meteor F Mk I aircraft established at RAF Manston in Kent in July 1944. Because of their greater speed, these aircraft were used to chase and destroy V-1 flying bombs by shooting them down over the sea or open countryside before they could reach their targets further inland.

In August 1944, after all four of his guns had jammed, Flying Officer Dean manoeuvred his aircraft alongside a V-1 and used the disturbed airflow from his wing tip to flip the flying bomb over, causing it to crash. This was the first destruction of a V-1 by a jet fighter; the squadron also destroyed a second flying bomb on the same day.

The improved Meteor III joined the squadron in December 1944 and in April 1945 the squadron took part in the first offensive operation by RAF jet aircraft when they attacked the Luftwaffe airfield at Nordholz from Belgium.

▲ Meteor F Mk.III of No. 616 Squadron, in Belgium, 1945.

A New Dawn

Preparing for Peace

Many changes took place following the cessation of hostilities. During 1946, RAF Reserve Command was formed and it was announced that the Auxiliary Air Force was to be re-established and organised into 13 day-fighter, 3 night-fighter and 4 light-bomber squadrons. The Air Ministry decided that the RAF Regiment would continue as an organic part of the RAF, and would comprise a number of rifle, armoured car and light anti-aircraft (LAA) squadrons. Some units of the RAF Regiment would also become parachute capable. As the service was scaled down from its wartime status, it was reduced from 1,100,000 to around 358,000 personnel by the end of June 1946.

Changes in organisation within the service in the late 1940s and 1950s included the formation of the Women's RAF (WRAF) on 1 February 1949, which replaced the Women's Auxiliary Air Force

(WAAF). Female emancipation within the RAF was demonstrated when, on 20 September 1952, Pilot Officer Jean Lennox Bird of the Women's RAF Volunteer Reserve became the first woman to be awarded RAF pilot's wings.

After the end of the war in Europe, the RAF assisted the British Army in maintaining order within the British Zone of occupation, and was tasked with supervising the dissolution of the Luftwaffe. The formal state of war between Britain and Germany ended officially on 9 July 1951.

Since then, the RAF has continued to be involved in airlifting troops and supplies in support of British, Allied, and Commonwealth forces in a series of operations around the world that have continued sporadically into the 21st century. During the 1950s, the RAF was called upon several times to deliver troops and equipment and to take part in operations in trouble spots in various parts of the world.

Far East

The ending of the war against Japan
did not result in a peaceful time for
the RAF as far as the Far East was
concerned. In September 1945, the
RAF South East Asia Command
established an Air Headquarters in the
Dutch East Indies to oversee the RAF's
involvement in the repatriation of Allied
internees. The RAF helped to ensure
that the nationalist forces of the newly
declared Republic of Indonesia did not
disrupt the process. This involvement
continued with 19,533 sorties flown in
that campaign, until it was gradually
wound down before eventually ceasing
at the end of November 1946.

Trouble was also brewing in French
Indo-China, the present-day Vietnam.
Following its deployment to Tan
Son Nhut airfield at Saigon, No 273
Squadron flew armed sorties in their
Spitfire Mk 9 aircraft in support of
British troops in the French colony.
They were joined at their new base
by a flight of Mosquito PR 34 aircraft
from No 684 Squadron engaged on
photo-mapping duties. Douglas Dakota
transports of No 267 Squadron also

Middle East

It was not long before the RAF was once again in action in the Middle East. This time the Aden Protectorate was the focus of attention. In February 1947, after local unrest, a fort occupied by dissidents was attacked by a force of RAF Regiment armoured cars in support of ground troops belonging to the Aden Protectorate Levies. Mosquitoes of No 8 Squadron gave aerial support in the form of rocket attacks. Further skirmishes took place on several occasions during the year and culminated in the almost total destruction of the village of Thumier in October. In an effort to avoid civilian casualties a leaflet drop giving warning of impending action preceded the attack. No 8 Squadron, by now equipped with Hawker Tempest ground attack aircraft, and supported by Lincoln bombers from No 101 Squadron, carried out the raid. The actions by dissidents continued at intervals throughout the next 20 years, leading to the eventual withdrawal of all British forces from Aden by 1967.

The RAF in the Middle East suffered the destruction of some of its aircraft and damage to others in a series of

operated from the Tan Son Nhut base, together with a unit of Japanese transport aircraft designated Gremlin Force. These were flown by Japanese crews under British command in support of British and French ground forces. The Gremlin Force flew over 2,000 sorties before being disbanded in January 1946.

terrorist attacks on bases in Palestine during February 1947. In one of these attacks, seven Spitfires, eleven Halifaxes and two Ansons were destroyed or damaged beyond economical repair on a single night. There were also frequent attacks on British military patrols and transport outside the bases, causing damage to vehicles and disruption to British Army and RAF movements.

In a rapidly deteriorating situation, Operation Polly was initiated in order to evacuate all non-essential civilians. In two days, Halifax transport aircraft from No 113 Squadron evacuated 508 people to Egypt. Following the partitioning of the former Palestine and the establishment of the new state of Israel, the RAF began to withdraw from its bases in the area. During the latter stages of the withdrawal, the Egyptian Air Force carried out three separate attacks, in error, on the RAF airfield at Ramat David. During these attacks, ten Spitfires from Nos 32 and 208 Squadrons were damaged, two being totally destroyed. A Dakota from No 204 Squadron was also destroyed and a further two damaged, as were three Austers. Four of the attackers were shot down by RAF Spitfires, and a

▲ Living quarters at RAF Station El Firdan, Egypt, 1953.

◀ RAF truck overturned and set alight during disturbances in Allenby Road, Tel Aviv, August 1947.

fifth by anti-aircraft fire.

Trouble flared, again in the Middle East towards the end of 1956. Israel had attacked bases within Sinai in Egypt, from where Egyptian forces had raided Israel. Following an ultimatum issued by Britain and France to the two adversaries that was accepted by Israel but rejected by Egypt, the RAF once more took to the skies in the Middle East. Canberra and Valiant bombers carried out bombing raids on twelve Egyptian airfields in the Nile Delta and the Canal Zone. This series of raids included the first operational use of a V-bomber, albeit in a conventional role, and successfully neutralised the Egyptian Air Force while it was on the ground.

RAF aircraft continued operations in support of ground troops and, together with aircraft of both the French Air Force and their naval comrades Aeronavale, carried out further attacks on targets in preparation for an amphibious assault on Port Said in November. In December, a United Nations peacekeeping force took over in the Canal Zone prior to the withdrawal of British and French forces.

Berlin Airlift

In June 1948 the Soviets initiated a military blockade on all land and water routes through the Russian Zone of Germany, effectively isolating the western-controlled sector of Berlin. This left only three 20-mile wide air corridors over Russian territory that could be used to supply the inhabitants. The Allies were faced with the stark choice of allowing the inhabitants of Berlin to starve or attempting to supply them with basic necessities by air. In choosing the latter, they were faced with a mammoth task.

The first day of Operation Vittles began on 26 June 1948 when United States Air Force (USAF) Dakotas delivered a meagre 80 tons of food to the beleaguered city. This was only a fraction of the estimated daily requirement for 4,500 tons of food, coal and other goods necessary to ensure the survival of the 2.5 million inhabitants. It was not known at the time that this effort would need to be sustained for a period of eleven months.

Two days later, RAF Dakota transport aircraft of No 46 Group began to supply the British military garrison in Berlin in Operation Knicker. On the following day supplies for the civilian population began to be delivered in Operation Carter Patterson, a name the Russians knew well as belonging to a British removals company of that time. To dispel any thoughts the Russians might have had about the possibility of a withdrawal by Britain, on 3 July the name was changed to Operation Plainfare, a play on words that was particularly appropriate. On the same day, RAF Avro York transport aircraft

flew their first missions into Berlin. Two days later, they were joined in the airlift by Sunderland flying boats of Nos 201 and 230 Squadrons, Coastal Command, flying between Hamburg and the Haval See, a large lake situated within the boundaries of Berlin.

The Soviets did their best to disrupt the airlift. In spite of being harassed by Russian fighters, barrage balloons being set loose across the air lanes, and the jamming of radio signals, the airlift was successful in more than just its primary

▼ Handley Page Hastings being unloaded in the British Sector of Berlin, 1949.

▲ Vampire and Meteor aircraft undergoing maintenance in the Canal Zone of Egypt, 1956.

cargo aircraft for both military and civilian purposes; this resulted in the development by the Americans of the C-130, C-141 and C-5 aircraft types.

At times aircraft were landing in Berlin at a rate of one every three minutes, and during the airlift a total of 2.3 million tons of aid from 277,569 flights was delivered. The RAF delivered 281,727 short tons of freight into Berlin, flew 29,532 short tons out to the West, and carried 67,373 passengers. The Lancastrian, York, and Hastings transport aircraft, and the Sunderlands of Coastal Command, altogether flew 18,205,284 miles during 49,733 sorties. Although the Russians lifted the blockade on 12 May 1949, the airlift continued until September of that year in order to create a stockpile of supplies.

Korea

Following the outbreak of the Korean War in 1950, No 88 Squadron commenced maritime reconnaissance operations with Sunderland flying boats from Iwakuni in Japan in support of the United Nations blockade of North Korea. Further Sunderland operations were carried out on monthly rotation

objective. One of the lessons learned by the Allies in the co-ordination and close control of air traffic led to the subsequent establishment of the civil 'airways' corridor system that is now used throughout the world. Also, the standardisation of aircraft loading and unloading procedures, and other benefits resulting from mutual operations, could be put into use in later humanitarian relief scenarios. The airlift also highlighted the need for dedicated with Nos 205 and 209 Squadrons until 31 July 1953. Hastings transport aircraft from No 53 Squadron began casualty evacuation flights between Iwakuni and the UK in September 1950.

Although no RAF combat aircraft were involved in the Korean conflict, a total of 32 RAF pilots took part when they were attached to No 77 Squadron Royal Australian Air Force (RAAF). Officially they were on secondment to help train Australian pilots in using the ex-RAF Meteor F8 fighters that had been acquired by the RAAF. Of the RAF pilots, four were killed in action, one was killed in a flying accident and one, Flying Officer M O Berg, became a prisoner of war when forced to eject from his Gloster Meteor F8 after it had been damaged by anti-aircraft fire. Four RAF pilots were awarded the Distinguished Flying Cross, six were Mentioned in Dispatches, and four were decorated with Air Medals by the United States.

Elsewhere in the Korean War, 21 RAF pilots served on attachment with either the 4th or the 51st Fighter Interceptor Wings of the USAF. Of these, four failed to return from

▲ Pilot of No. 8 Squadron pictured in his Vampire fighter in Kenya, 1954.

operational sorties. Each of the RAF pilots damaged one or more North Korean Mikoyan-Gurevich MiG15s in combat. One pilot, Squadron Leader G S Hulse, was credited with achieving two kills before failing to return from a sortie on 13 March 1953; a further five were credited with one kill each.

New Aircraft

The years following the end of World War II saw a variety of aircraft types enter into service with the RAF. Of these, some were later versions of aircraft that had seen wartime service and others were developments or adaptations of existing designs; a comparatively small number were completely new designs.

The Spitfire Mk 21 entered service in 1945, as did the Hawker Tempest II and the Sikorski Hoverfly, the first helicopter to be operated by the RAF. The latest version of the comparatively new jet fighter, the Gloster Meteor III, joined No 74 Squadron in the forefront of Britain's air defence duties. Two developments of the Lancaster bomber, the Avro Lincoln bomber and the Lancastrian transport, were also added to the inventory of RAF aircraft.

In January 1947, one of the more 'shiny' aircraft entered service with the delivery of the first Vickers Viking to The King's Flight at RAF Benson in Oxfordshire. New fighter aircraft came on stream with the arrival of the first de Havilland Vampire F1 fighters with No 247 Squadron, which was to be based at RAF Odiham in Hampshire for the next decade.

During 1948, No 47 Squadron became the first RAF transport squadron to receive the Handley Page Hastings C1, just in time to be pressed into service on the Berlin Airlift. Carrying mainly coal, the squadron flew over 3,000 sorties in seven months. The Gloster Meteor T7 also joined up in 1948 for the start of its lengthy service career. Initially with No 203 Advanced Flying School, the Meteor T7 served with a great number of RAF units as testified by the 642 aircraft ordered by the Ministry of Supply, and a further 40 by overseas customers.

In 1949, the Bristol Brigand first appeared in RAF service with No 84 Squadron, and was involved in counter-terrorist strikes against insurgents during Operation Firedog in Malaya. However, due to a number of accidents, the Brigand was grounded and withdrawn from service. The same year saw the entry into RAF service of yet another stalwart, the de Havilland Devon, on communications duties at RAF Hendon with No 31 Squadron. The Vickers Valetta became a workhorse with transport squadrons both at home and overseas.

The 1950s saw the entry into service of another great aircraft, favourite of many RAF pilots, the de Havilland Chipmunk two-seat trainer. The 'Chippy' was probably the first aircraft in which many future RAF pilots flew. University Air Squadrons, where many pilots learned to fly on scholarships awarded by the RAF, were among those who used the Chipmunk. It was also used extensively for flying Air Training Corps Cadets on air experience flights, which often resulted in the use of the paper bag that was provided for the aftermath of an 'aerobatics initiation' ceremony!

The helicopter inventory saw the introduction of the Westland Dragonfly, a licence-built version of the Sikorski S-51, and it was soon put to work in the war against terrorists in Malaya. The much-improved Meteor F8 and FR 9 variants also entered service from 1950.

The RAF needed a 'stop-gap' aircraft to replace the aging Lincoln bomber pending the delivery of new jet-powered bombers. The first crews from No 115 Squadron commenced training on the Boeing B-29 in the USA in March 1950. The first batch of 87 aircraft, designated Washington Mk 1 by the RAF, later arrived at RAF Marham in Norfolk, flown by their newly trained crews.

Britain's night fighter capability was entrusted to the Armstrong-Whitworth

▲ Sixteen Hawker Hunters from No. 111 Squadron, who performed a formation 'loop' with 22 aircraft at the Farnborough Air Show in 1958.

▲ English
Electric Canberra
B2. Britain's first
jet bomber.

Meteor NF11s, some of which joined No 29 Squadron in 1951. Maritime reconnaissance duties were taken over by the Avro Shackleton. The 'Shack' was to remain in service in several incarnations for many years to come. Another 'stop-gap' from the USA filled the maritime patrol requirement prior to the arrival of the Shackleton in the guise of the Lockheed Neptune MR Mk 1.

The advent of the English Electric Canberra heralded yet another aircraft type that would give valuable and lengthy service in the RAF. In a number of roles

and in several variants, the Canberra remained in RAF service for almost half a century. Meanwhile, RAF Germany was the destination for the first two squadrons of Canadian-built Sabre fighters and, out of a total of 427 Sabre F4s delivered, the majority served in eleven German-based RAF squadrons with only two squadrons of Sabres being based in the UK.

The Supermarine Swift fighter aircraft was ordered as a 'fall-back' in case the Hawker Hunter project failed. With the benefit of hindsight,

▲ De Havilland Comet.

it was the Swift that failed to live up to its publicity. Except for it breaking the world absolute speed record over Libya on 26 September 1953 with a speed of 735mph, the Swift was generally considered to be less than a success as a fighter. It later regained some respectability as a fighter-reconnaissance aircraft.

In stark contrast, the Hawker Hunter was a remarkable asset to the RAF in both the fighter and ground-attack roles. This good-looking aircraft attracted the attention of all those who saw it, either in flight or on the ground. Few who witnessed the event could forget the sight of 22 Hunters in a formation 'loop' at Farnborough in 1958, described in *Flight* magazine as: "... the most wonderful mass aerobatic manoeuvre

▲ Gloster
Javelin.

ever witnessed at Farnborough (or, we are moved to declare, elsewhere)."

The Gloster Javelin assumed the mantle of the all-weather fighter when it entered service with No 46 Squadron in 1956. The middle years of the decade saw even more newcomers to RAF service: the Blackburn Beverley and the de Havilland Comet transport aircraft were at opposite ends of the aesthetic spectrum, but both proved valuable assets in their differing roles. These were augmented by the arrival in service of the Bristol Britannia in 1959.

Between 1955 and 1959 the RAF received the aircraft it needed to fulfil its strategic bombing capability as the triumvirate of V-bombers began to enter service. Early in 1955 came the eight Vickers Valiant B1s, followed in July 1957 by the first Avro Vulcan B1s, and the Handley Page Victor B1 entered service late in 1957.

The RAF was now ready for any action that might be necessary if the Cold War situation should deteriorate to such a level that retaliatory strikes would become a reality. However, with a view to its history, the predecessor of the Battle of Britain Memorial Flight (BBMF) was formed at RAF Biggin Hill in Kent in July 1957. The Historic Aircraft Flight, as it was then known, received three Spitfire PR Mk 19 aircraft in addition to its Hurricane LF363.

White Paper And White Bombers

The Defence White Paper – 1957

The disbanding of the Royal Auxiliary Air Force in March 1957 was the first in a series of political decisions that had a somewhat demoralising effect on the members of the RAF.

In April 1957, the government issued a White Paper on Defence that was to have a far-reaching effect on Britain's defence industry as a whole, and a particular effect on the RAF. The political view of the Conservative government of the day was that in the future Britain should place far greater reliance on a strategic nuclear deterrent than on conventional military strength and posturing. Of particular pertinence to the RAF was the premise that all manned aircraft could be replaced by

guided missiles by the year 1970. With this philosophy, most existing aircraft development projects could, therefore, be cancelled and the defence of Britain would be vested in the deterrent effect of its nuclear weapons.

The plans outlined in the White Paper were based on the UK armed forces having a total strength of 380,000 regular personnel. The RAF was to have a strength of 135,000 regular adult males. The moderate-sized bomber force was to be replaced by ballistic rockets with a stock of British-made nuclear bombs supplemented by American bombs, the use of which was to be subject to US control. The air defence of Great Britain was to be 280 fighters (versus the 480 in service in 1957) limited to the task of protecting bomber bases, and to be largely replaced in due course by guided missiles.

▲ Aircrew
pictured on the
Canberra flight
line at RAF
Bassingbourne,
Cambridgeshire,
1952.

Coastal Command was to be reduced in strength from twelve to seven squadrons and Transport Command was to be reduced in strength to seven and a half squadrons, including 16 Britannias and 32 Beverleys. Tactical Air Force in Germany was to reduce in strength from 466 aircraft in 1957, initially to 216 and then to 104 by 1961. Some four squadrons of Canberras for assignment to Supreme Allied Commander Europe would be based in the UK.

In the Near East and Middle East, four light-bomber squadrons, one transport squadron and one photo-reconnaissance squadron were to be stationed in Cyprus, along with four squadrons at Aden and one maritime squadron at Malta. The Far East Air Force was to go from 134 to 74 aircraft, including one light-bomber squadron, one fighter-bomber squadron, one maritime reconnaissance squadron, one photo-reconnaissance squadron and three transport squadrons. The fighter squadron in Hong Kong was to be withdrawn.

Some of the reasoning used in the decision-making process leading to the White Paper appears to have been flawed. The cost savings obtained in the resultant withdrawal or reduction in forces from some overseas commitments are undeniable. However, elsewhere in the world other governments, including those of France, the United States and the Soviet Union, were already investing in advanced defence programmes.

Of the few remaining defence projects, the English Electric Lightning fighter, while being supersonic in level flight without using its reheat and having a high rate of climb, was hampered by its relatively short range. This necessitated installation of an in-flight refuelling probe in order to

provide a respectable radius of operation. Pilots who flew the Lightning were generally enthusiastic about the aircraft, notwithstanding its shortcomings in range. Its maintenance crews were less than impressed, largely due to its tightly packed equipment and their unfamiliarity with a complex aircraft and systems. This was compounded by the lack of foresight by planners in failing to provide sufficient training facilities and support systems.

Within a few years, despite its early difficulties, the Lightning had evolved into a potent defender of Britain's skies. When introduced into the RAF with a

▲ Lightning F1 fighters in formation.

planned service life of ten years, it was seen as being little more than a token gesture before manned aircraft were replaced by guided missiles, but the Lightning continued in service with the RAF until 1988.

The Nuclear Deterrent

The RAF carried out its first trial drop of an atomic weapon in October 1956 at the Maralinga weapons range in South Australia. A Vickers Valiant of No 49 Squadron released a Blue Danube round with a yield of between three and four kilotons from an altitude of 30,000 feet.

Blue Danube was the first operational British nuclear weapon; it also went by a variety of other names including Smallboy, the Mk 1 Atom Bomb, and OR1001, a reference to the Operational Requirement that called for such a weapon. It was intended as the primary armament of the V-bomber force and the bomb bays of the V-bomber aircraft had been designed specifically to hold it. The Blue Danube weapon was declared fit for operations in November 1953. In April 1954, a

Vickers Valiant unit was established at RAF Wittering in Cambridgeshire to integrate the Blue Danube nuclear weapon into RAF service.

In May 1957, the first of a series of tests known as Operation Grapple took place from Christmas Island in the Pacific and a Vickers Valiant successfully dropped a Yellow Sun thermonuclear weapon with a yield of 100 to 150 kilotons. In all nine nuclear detonations took place in the air rather than on the surface to reduce the effects of fallout.

Air Defence Missiles

In development since 1947, the Bristol Bloodhound surface to air missile began to be deployed operationally in December 1958. There were shortcomings in its effectiveness, not least being an inadequate range of around 50 miles and problems with its pulsed radar system being vulnerable to jamming. The fact that Bloodhound was designed to operate from a fixed base meant that lack of launch-site flexibility was also a disadvantage. The Bloodhound Mk 2, deployed in the mid-1960s with a range of around 115 miles, overcame most of these problems

◀ RAF Gaydon, Warwickshire in 1956. Chief Technician L. Paddock, the aircraft crew chief, standing beneath the tail of a Vickers Valiant.

but still operated from a fixed base.

The premise that the defence of V-bomber bases could be carried out solely by using guided missiles was erroneous. This placed even greater reliance on manned RAF fighters and their supporting air defence and ground-based radar systems in the prevention a potential attacker from entering British airspace. In practical terms there was little defence against any attack by a strategic missile other than the corresponding 'deterrent' of nuclear retaliation against the aggressor.

Strategic Nuclear Weapons

The RAF entered the strategic nuclear missile arena in 1958 following an agreement with the United States in which the USA would supply 60 Douglas Thor Intermediate Range Ballistic Missiles (IRBMs) and their warheads to Britain for a period of five years. The first RAF Thor-equipped missile squadron was formed at RAF Feltwell in Norfolk in September 1958 to develop RAF Thor missile maintenance and launch procedures, albeit without any missiles at this time.

Launching of the missiles was to

be controlled by means of a coded authentication command and a 'dual key' missile firing and warhead arming protocol. RAF and USAF officers held the dual keys jointly. The British key could initiate a launch: however, the USAF key retained the arming of the warhead under United States control.

As early as 1954 it had been recognised that it would be dangerous for the proposed V-bombers to overfly or approach within 50 miles of their targets because of medium-range missile defences. Contracts were placed for the development of a guided bomb that would allow the launching V-bomber to 'stand off' from its target. The bomb was to carry a British nuclear warhead. The fact that no suitable warhead was available for three to five years coupled with other problems in development delayed the entry of 'Blue Steel' into RAF service until 1962. Blue Steel replaced the Thor IRBM as Britain's nuclear deterrent. Around 36 V-bombers were made 'Blue Steel capable', serving until 1969 when Britain's nuclear deterrent was passed to the Royal Navy's Polaris submarine-launched ballistic missile.

Following the cancellation of the British Blue Streak intercontinental ballistic missile programme in 1960, the British government agreed to purchase the GAM-87 Skybolt long-range air-launched ballistic missile (ALBM), which would be carried by Vulcan B2 aircraft. In 1962, after a series of economic and political problems, the United States cancelled the Skybolt project.

Tactical Nuclear Weapons

Tactical nuclear weapons are designed to be used on a battlefield as part of an attack with conventional forces. As well as being deployed in the UK and Germany, tactical nuclear weapons were deployed as early as 1960 at RAF Akrotiri on one of Britain's Sovereign Base Areas in southern Cyprus. Two years later Prime Minister Harold Macmillan personally authorised the storage of nuclear weapons at RAF Tengah in Singapore.

By 1960 an area within the RAF base at Akrotiri had been readied for the operational storage of up to 16 Red Beard tactical nuclear weapons.

The following year permanent storage facilities for a further 32 of these weapons were opened nearby at Cape Gata. Airfield facilities at Akrotiri were upgraded to handle the Vulcan bombers that arrived in 1962 and were to remain based there until 1975.

The RAF was also making plans for the arrival in Singapore of 48 Red Beard weapons at RAF Tengah in 1962. Canberras based at the station were capable of delivering Red Beard using the LABS (Low Altitude Bombing System) toss-bombing technique, and this remained the primary means of tactical nuclear weapons delivery until around 1970, when the Tengah base was

▲ RAF crew training with a Skybolt missile at USAF base at Eglin, Florida, in 1962.

◀ RAF Fylingdales's early warning radar inside its protective Golf Ball'.

de-activated as an RAF station.

These activities were carried out in great secrecy, and the British government chose not to inform the respective heads of the countries about them. In a since-declassified memorandum from 1960, an official in the Air Ministry insisted that all those involved maintain their silence: "All possible measures should be taken in Cyprus to conceal the arrival and storage of nuclear bombs, whether they be inert or drill or the real McCoy."

The WE177 became operational in late 1966, replacing Red Beard, and was destined to be the last air-launched atomic bomb in the UK's inventory. It was a free-fall thermonuclear weapon carried by the Vulcan, Buccaneer, Jaguar, Harrier and Tornado. It also formed the basis for a nuclear depth charge that was deployed on vessels of the Royal Navy.

The Vulcan

The Vulcan Operational Conversion Unit (OCU) was formed at RAF Waddington in Lincolnshire in 1955 and received its first aircraft in July 1956. The OCU took part in a series of record-breaking flights around the world that had the dual effects of waving the Union Flag and drawing attention to Britain's nuclear capability. Flights from Waddington to Boston, USA, in 5 hours and 17 minutes and to Cyprus in 3 hours and 41 minutes showed the world that the RAF had a fast and effective means of delivering a retaliatory strike.

By 1959 there were three Vulcan squadrons, and selection criteria for the Vulcan aircrew were stringent: pilots were required to have at least 1,750 flying hours and an 'above average' proficiency rating, while co-pilots needed to have amassed at least 700 hours. Navigators and Air Electronics Officers (AEOs) were required to be 'experienced'.

Life on the V-bomber squadrons was punctuated by the frequent number of exercises that tested their readiness for action at short notice. In addition to scramble alerts, there were often station alertness exercises that involved all personnel in a 'stand-to' at some deliberately chosen, anti-social time of day, usually in the early morning hours. Known as 'Mick', these exercises required the generation of the maximum number of serviceable aircraft and arming them within as short a period as possible, culminating in a 'crew in' situation in which engines were sometimes started. This state fell short of the full-scale 'Mickey Finn' scenario, in which the aircraft were ordered to take off and proceed to a nominated dispersed site at any of the 36 airfields around the UK.

Living in temporary accommodation near their aircraft, the crew members awaited the scramble call. When received, the Vulcan crews ran to their pre-checked aircraft, the AEO boarded first in order to start his equipment and was followed in sequence by the two pilots and then the two navigators. Engines were started while the crew strapped in, with the object of getting the aircraft onto the runway within two minutes. In most practice situations the aircraft were not carrying a nuclear weapon.

◀ Avro Vulcan.

Along with the continuation of the usually annual 'Mickey Finn' dispersal exercises, a permanent V-bomber Quick Reaction Alert (QRA) capability was established in 1962; this required at least one aircraft from each operational squadron to be at 15 minutes' readiness at all times.

The Victor

Deliveries of the Handley Page Victor B1 bomber began in November 1957, when No 232 OCU became the first RAF unit to be equipped with this type. The following April No 10 Squadron became the first squadron to become

WHITE PAPER AND WHITE BOMBERS

with the Yellow Sun nuclear weapon, until the mid-1960s when its role was fundamentally changed.

As the Victor B2 version was entering service there was a shift in policy from high-altitude bombing to the low-level, under-the-radar method of attack. The additional stresses imposed at low-level had caused the onset of severe fatigue problems in the Valiant bombers that had also carried out the bulk of RAF air-to-air refuelling duties. The tanker availability situation became critically compromised when, in January 1965, it was discovered that the main spars in the Valiant airframes were seriously fatigued after performing low-level duties for which they had not been designed, and all Valiants were immediately grounded.

Faced with a shortage of tanker capability, it was decided to hurriedly convert six of the Victor B1As to the 'two-point' tanker role. These were fitted with in-flight refuelling pods, one under each wing: later aircraft were fitted with an additional centreline pod and became known as 'three-point' tankers. With the advent of the Victor B2 into operational bombing duties, the earlier versions

◀ Handley Page Victor B2 in antiflash white colour scheme with its crew and Blue Steel stand-off bomb at RAF Wittering, Northants, 1964.

operationally ready. The Victor's bomb bay was significantly larger than that of the other two V-bomber types, a feature demonstrated when it successfully carried and later dropped a total of thirty-five 1,000lb bombs at one time. The Victor B1 and B1A versions continued in service, often being armed

The TSR-2

The TSR-2 was to be a 'cutting-edge of technology'Tactical/Strike/Reconnaissance (TSR) aircraft that was designed as a replacement for the Canberra bomber. The project was intended to provide an aircraft that could penetrate enemy airspace at low level and at very high speeds. It was to carry the most advanced avionics suite in the world, including Doppler radar, terrain-following radar integrated with the flight control system, ground mapping radar and a head-up flight-instrument display. The TSR-2 was designed to be capable of delivering a large payload of conventional or nuclear weapons with greater accuracy and with greater mission survivability than any comparable aircraft envisaged at that time. The prototype had flown early in 1965, and the test flight programme was progressing well. The second prototype was almost ready to join the test programme when the project was cancelled along with several other defence projects, including new aircraft carriers for the Royal Navy.

It was to be many years before the RAF would receive a single aircraft type that could perform all of the functions that the TSR-2 promised.

that had been modified as tankers were re-designated K1 and K1A. Thus began a lengthy association with the airborne tanker role that was to last for almost 30 years, with the Victor K2s taking over from their earlier stable-mates. The Victor aircraft finally ended its service in 1993, with the disbandment of No 55 Squadron at RAF Marham in Norfolk.

The Victor also proved to be a fine reconnaissance aircraft. Nine B2s were converted during build to become B(SR)2 aircraft. These were used for strategic reconnaissance duties, a role they performed for some eight years, following which three of their number underwent a metamorphosis to emerge as tankers.

The 60s And 70s

Flash Points
And Confrontation

During the 1960s the RAF found itself involved in a range of roles in flash points and conflicts around the world. In 1961 and 1962 it provided troop, supplies and equipment transport and support for peacekeeping activities in the Congo and Cameroon, and as a military deterrent against Iraqi threats to Kuwait, North Vietnamese incursions in Thailand, and rebellion in Brunei. RAF support of counter-insurgency operations against Indonesian-sponsored rebels in Malaysia began towards the latter part of 1963 and lasted for almost four years.

The RAF was also prominent in operations in the Middle East, as tensions heightened in the Aden Protectorate in 1964, and the RAF and Fleet Air Arm gave air support to British Army units in the Radfan area. By March the conflict had escalated to the extent that armed helicopters

from the Yemen, supported by MiG–17 fighters, crossed the border and attacked the village of Bulaq and a frontier guard post. RAF Hunters carried out a retaliatory raid, destroying a Yemeni fort. In the following three months the Hunters flew 642 sorties in support of ground forces, firing 2,508 rockets and 183,900 rounds of ammunition in the process. Shackletons carrying out night bombing attacks also flew support missions, while Beverley transport aircraft together with Belvedere and Whirlwind helicopters provided airlift and tactical transport for both ground troops and their supplies.

In November 1967 British withdrawal from Aden was to become the largest airlift operation carried out by the RAF since the Berlin Airlift of 1948-49. A total of 5,800 British Army personnel were flown out to RAF Muharraq in the Persian Gulf in a fleet of Hercules, Britannia and Belfast aircraft of Transport Command. All locally based units were either relocated

◀ The prototype TSR-2 that was a victim of cuts in defence spending, 1965.

▲ Hawker Hunter and ground crew at RAF Biggin Hill.

to bases within the Middle East or disbanded; the withdrawal from Aden was completed by 29 November 1967.

Meanwhile, RAF units were also occupied in transporting British troops sent in response to requests for assistance from the governments of Tanganyika, Uganda and Kenya where, in January 1964, there had been a mutiny by five battalions of local troops.

In response to a Unilateral Declaration of Independence (UDI) by the Rhodesian government in 1965, Britain attempted to blockade the illegal regime, which also required it to provide support to Zambia's economy in the form of supplying oil and petroleum products by airlift from Dar-Es-Salaam in Tanzania, Leopoldville in the Congo and Nairobi in Kenya, as rail link formerly used for the transport of such supplies from Mozambique passed through Rhodesian territory.

Assisted by Canadian forces, the airlift carried over 3.5 million gallons of oil products into Zambia. RAF Britannias of Nos 99 and 511 Squadrons and Hastings of Nos 24 and 36 Squadrons participated in the airlift, which ended in October 1966. Shackletons of Nos 37, 38, 42, 204 and 210 Squadrons, on rotation, assisted the Royal Navy in enforcing a blockade of the port of Beira in Mozambique from March 1966 to February 1972.

At home in Britain, an unusual operation involving Hunter aircraft from RAF Chivenor in Devon and RAF West Raynham in Norfolk took place at the end of March 1967. Together with Buccaneers from the Fleet Air Arm they took part in a series of rocket and bomb attacks on the tanker *Torrey Canyon* that had run aground on rocks

▲ Vulcan B2
shortly after
takeoff.

of the Seven Stones reef near Land's End in Cornwall. The mission was to attempt to destroy the major part of the cargo of 120,000 tons of crude oil that was causing severe pollution both in the sea and on nearby beaches.

Northern Ireland was to become the focus of attention for RAF helicopter operations during the greater part of the next decade, with the arrival in the province of No 72 Squadron with their Westland Wessex helicopters in August 1970. The first RAF squadron to operate Puma helicopters, No 33 Squadron, also served prominently in this theatre.

From May to November 1973 RAF aircraft undertook fishery surveillance flights over Icelandic waters in what became known as the 'Second Cod War'. Generally, Nimrod aircraft undertook these patrols, but to conserve airframe

hours on the Nimrods, Britannia transport aircraft also carried out some patrols. In November 1975, RAF Nimrod aircraft once again helped in the protection of British fishing vessels within the unilaterally-declared 200-mile fishing prohibition zone around Iceland.

With the invasion of Northern Cyprus by Turkish troops in July 1974, British air defences in Cyprus were strengthened by the arrival of Phantom FGR2s of Nos 6 and 41 Squadrons and No 228 OCU, and RAF Regiment personnel from No 15 and 26 Squadrons to bolster the defence of ground installations and RAF bases.

Following heightened tensions between Guatemala and Britain over the status of Belize, RAF Puma helicopters were flown to the colony in Belfast heavy-lift transport aircraft in October

▶ Wessex helicopter supporting British troops in Aden, 1966.

1975. Further strengthening of defences, in order to deter any invasion by Guatemala, resulted in No 1 Squadron Harriers also being detached to Belize until the situation had normalised. In 1977, following another breakdown in negotiations between Guatemala and Britain, the Harriers of No 1 Squadron returned to Belize with the assistance of Victor tankers.

Some RAF aircraft ended the 1970s as part of a cease-fire monitoring force in Rhodesia. Seven Hercules aircraft from No 47 and 70 Squadrons and six Puma helicopters from No 33 Squadron took part. Tragically, one of the Pumas and its crew were lost when it flew into overhead cables only one day before the cease-fire came into effect.

Humanitarian And Relief Operations

During the period from 1961 to 1979 the RAF carried out a variety of relief operations resulting from natural disasters such as floods and the aftermath of hurricanes and cyclones. In many locations around the world, from high in the Himalayas to the deserts of the

Sahara, RAF aircraft and personnel have been in the forefront of humanitarian efforts to ease the suffering of both the hungry and the homeless.

October 1961 saw the combined efforts of RAF Transport Command and other Middle East-based units in Operation Tana. This involved the dropping of food supplies to communities that were isolated by floods, first in Kenya and then later in Somalia. The following month Operation Sky Help called upon the RAF to spring into action once again by carrying essential supplies between Kingston in Jamaica and Belize, after Hurricane Hattie had devastated large parts of British Honduras.

In November 1970 and again in June 1971 relief efforts were put into operation to aid the population of East Pakistan (now Bangladesh). Following cyclones that resulted in heavy flooding along the coastal areas, the RAF mounted an emergency airlift of food and medical supplies into Chittagong. This operation involved the Hercules transport aircraft of No 48 Squadron from their base at in Singapore, and was the first time this type of aircraft

had been used for such a purpose by the RAF. The ubiquitous Hercules, this time from RAF Lyneham in Wiltshire, took to the mountains of Nepal during March 1973. Because of famine in West Nepal and there being no suitable roads or airstrip, the dropping of emergency food supplies by air to the outlying villages was the only means of salvation for the population in this remote area.

In July 1974, following the invasion of Northern Cyprus by Turkish troops, RAF aircraft were used to evacuate British nationals and return them to the UK. The repatriation of service families followed in August, with a further evacuation of 9,989 dependants from RAF Akrotiri.

New Aircraft
And Equipment

Many new aircraft types or variants
entered service with the RAF during
the 1960s and 1970s. From the arrival of
the Lightning F1 with No 74 Squadron
in 1960, there followed a succession
of shiny debutantes onto the flight
lines of stations throughout the UK
and overseas. In 1961 two new types
of helicopter, the Westland Whirlwind
HAR 10 and the twin-rotor Bristol

Belvedere, entered service. The same
year saw the arrival of the Hunter FR 10,
the Victor B2 and the Jet Provost T4.

New types making their debut in
1962 were the de Havilland Comet
C4 and Armstrong Whitworth Argosy
transport aircraft, and the diminutive
Folland Gnat trainer. A new variant
of the Lightning, the F2, also entered
service. After a year of no change, 1964
was notable for the entry into service
of the Westland Wessex HC2 helicopter,
the Hawker Siddeley Andover CC2 for
The Queen's Flight and the Lightning

F3 for No 74 Squadron.

Although not entering RAF operational squadron service, the forerunner of the Harrier, the Hawker P1127 Kestrel, arrived at RAF West Raynham in Norfolk in 1964, where it joined a 'Tripartite Evaluation Squadron' to undergo trials by United Kingdom, German and United States forces.

The following year saw the Beagle Basset enter the hangar of the Northern Communications Squadron, the arrival of the Hawker Siddeley Dominie for No 1 Air Navigation School and the Lightning F6 for No 5 Squadron. In 1966 the latest incarnation of the Canberra, the T17 variant, was allocated to No 39 Squadron. Transport Command was boosted by the arrival of the Andover C1, the Vickers VC10 C1 and the Short Belfast that incorporated the infamous 'bandstand' passenger seating arrangement located on a 'mezzanine' floor from where the occupants were afforded a marvellous view of the cargo. In that year the service also began to receive the Short Tigercat airfield defence surface-to-air missile system for use by No 48 Squadron, RAF Regiment.

The first aircraft of a batch of 66 Lockheed C130K aircraft, known in the RAF as the Hercules C1, arrived in 1967 and the type has continued to serve into the 21st century. Also acquired from the USA, but intended for a completely different purpose, the first of 118 McDonnell Douglas Phantom FGR2s went into RAF service in 1968 with No 228 OCU, where crews were trained to fly this ground-attack and reconnaissance fighter.

The year 1969 saw aircraft types as varied as the Beagle Husky of No 5 Air Experience Flight, the Harrier GR1 of No 1 Squadron, the Jet Provost T5 of the Central Flying School and the Phantom FG1 of No 43 Squadron enter into service. They were joined by the Hawker Siddeley Buccaneer for No 12 Squadron and the 'mighty hunter' Nimrod from the same manufacturer for No 236 OCU. This spate of new machinery was followed by a lull until 1971 when the Westland Puma helicopter arrived at No 33 Squadron and the BAe125 CC1 executive twin jet set forth on the first of its VIP transport tasks with No 32 Squadron.

◀ Lightning F6.

▲ Ground crew at work on a Lightning T5 of No. 56 Squadron at RAF Akrotiri, Cyprus. (© Crown Copyright)

Air Arm Gannet AEW3. The aircraft was intended as a 'stop-gap' measure following delays in the Nimrod AEW project that were to lead to its eventual cancellation. This supposedly short-term solution was to last for almost 20 years.

The Central Flying School received two new types in 1973, the Westland Gazelle helicopter and the Scottish Aviation Bulldog, while No 5 Flying Training School acquired the Scottish Aviation Jetstream. Somewhat noisier, the SEPECAT Jaguar also began to make itself seen and heard in the skies around its new home, the Jaguar OCU at RAF Coltishall in Norfolk in 1974. In the same year No 51 Squadron received the first of its Nimrod R1 aircraft, at RAF Wyton in Cambridgeshire, where it joined the squadron's specially modified Canberra aircraft on signals surveillance duties.

In 1975 the tanker force was strengthened by the arrival of the Victor K2 tanker for No 55 Squadron at RAF Marham in Norfolk. A year later the first BAe Hawk T1 arrived at No 4 FTS at RAF Valley on Anglesey. New metal, in the shape of the Andover E3 radar calibration aircraft that was to

Having had many of its alleged 'forty-thousand rivets flying in loose formation' tightened and its airframe fitted with a prominent radar dome, the Avro Shackleton Airborne Early Warning (AEW) MR2 joined 'The Magic Roundabout' cast of characters at No 8 Squadron in 1972. Each of the squadron's aircraft carried the name of a character from the popular children's television programme of the era, including the appropriately named 'Mr. Rusty'. This AEW version of the Shackleton was fitted with an APS 20 surveillance radar system that had originally been used in the Fleet

become a regular sight on the approach paths of RAF airfields for many years to come, joined No 115 Squadron at RAF Benson in Oxfordshire.

During the latter years of the decade, deliveries of new aircraft types slowed to a trickle. When the Westland Sea King HAR3 joined No 202 Squadron in 1978, all airmen, whose favourite colour is yellow, warmly welcomed it on arrival. This helicopter type has since taken part in many life-saving missions during a career that has stretched into the 21st century.

Command And Organisation

The 1960s and 1970s saw many changes in the RAF's operational and organisational arrangements. The Ballistic Missile Early Warning System (BMEWS) station at RAF Fylingdales on the North York Moors was declared operational in September 1963 and commenced operations in January 1964. On 1 April of that year a unified Ministry of Defence was created. New names were given to

▲ SEPECAT Jaguar.

the existing components.

Reorganisations and disbandments were rife, both at home and in several overseas RAF commands. Amongst other changes, in April 1966 the RAF Airfield Construction Branch was disbanded, its personnel being either relocated in other RAF branches or transferring to the Army as members of the Royal Engineers.

January 1968 began with sweeping cuts in Britain's defences. These included the cancellation of the contract for 50 General Dynamics F111 aircraft to replace the already cancelled TSR-2, and the withdrawal of British forces from the Persian Gulf and the Far East by December 1971, as well as increasing the rate of the reduction in numbers of RAF personnel. However, the RAF would inherit most of the fixed-wing aircraft from the Fleet Air Arm, as the

Royal Navy carrier fleet was to be phased out.

Meanwhile, a series of realignments and mergers led to the formation of new and fewer RAF command. RAF Training Command was reborn with the merger of Flying Training and Technical Training Commands. The year also saw the disappearance of the titles of Bomber Command and Fighter Command, followed the year after by that of Coastal Command, as they were absorbed into RAF Strike Command. RAF Transport Command was also renamed RAF Air Support Command and given a wider responsibility in tactical support/assault roles in addition to its long-range strategic transport function.

The final withdrawal from RAF bases in the Far East led to the disbanding of the Far East Air Force in October 1971, while a similar fate awaited Air Forces Gulf in the December of that year. Following the Turkish invasion of Cyprus in the previous year, January 1975 saw major changes in Cyprus. All RAF fixed-wing assets were withdrawn to the UK and re-deployed within Strike Command, leaving RAF Akrotiri almost bereft of aircraft except

for the helicopters of No 84 Squadron and UK-based transport aircraft staging through en route to elsewhere. As the decade neared its close, so did the RAF's presence on the island of Malta: on 31 March 1979 it withdrew, ending an association that had lasted for 60 years.

▼ An aircraft being refuelled at RAF Gan, in the Maldives, 1962.

War And The
Peace Dividend

The Winds
Of Change

RAF Hercules made humanitarian relief flights in Ethiopia as part of Operation Bushel at the end of 1985. These provided an emergency airlift of food and other essential supplies following both famine and civil war. More than 2,000 sorties were flown to either air

drop or air land more than 32,000 tonnes of aid to the stricken area.

The RAF finally severed its connection with the sea when the Marine Branch was disbanded on 1 April 1986. This Branch had served for many years as part of the Search and Rescue (SAR) service, both in peacetime and in war, saving the lives of many pilots that had ditched or parachuted into the sea. Its vessels also provided safety patrols around coastal weapons ranges and target-towing facilities.

Although women in the RAF had previously served in its aircraft as cabin crew, a new policy statement made in Parliament on 20 July 1989 announced that females should be allowed to fly as aircrew in all categories in non-combat roles, including that of pilot. The restriction that precluded female aircrew from flying support helicopters and maritime reconnaissance aircraft was lifted during 1991, followed by the announcement in December 1991 that fast-jet seats would now be available to female pilots and navigators. Women have successfully trained for all of these aircrew roles.

In 1996 in Germany the last headquarters unit of the RAF on mainland Europe finally closed. The military rundown and subsequent withdrawal of the RAF from mainland Europe heralded a new peace throughout the continent.

Later in 1996 the RAF retired both the Buccaneer strike aircraft and the last of the Victors that had served first as a bomber and later a tanker for 36 years. The sole surviving 'women only' service organisation, the Women's RAF (WRAF), disbanded on 1 April 1994. Amalgamation and inter-service co-operation went hand in hand as the RAF Staff College at Bracknell closed and was replaced on the same site by the new Joint Services Command and Staff College.

The last remaining RAF station in Asia, RAF Sek Kong in the New Territories, Hong Kong, finally closed in January 1997 in preparation for the handover of Hong Kong to China. The

last flying RAF squadron in the Far East, No 28 Squadron, temporarily transferred to the Hong Kong civil airport until withdrawing from the area in June 1997.

The RAF Volunteer Reserve (RAFVR) was disbanded and members integrated into the Royal Auxiliary Air Force (RAuxAF) that was to become the sole RAF reserve force. At the same time, the Operations Support Branch was created to combine the existing specialist elements of air traffic control, fighter control, intelligence and the RAF Regiment together with the newly created 'flight operations' specialisation.

▲ Buccaneer landing on a Carrier.

◀ Hercules coming in to land.

New Aircraft For The 80s And 90s

On 16 December 1983 a preliminary agreement was signed for the development of a Future European Fighter Aircraft, which over a decade later became the Eurofighter Typhoon. The RAF bade farewell to its last serving Avro Vulcan on 31 March 1984 and later that year greeted the first two Tornado F2s.

Notable among the new aircraft entering RAF service during the 1980s were the Lockheed Hercules C3 transport aircraft and the Panavia Tornado GR1 combat aircraft in 1980, followed by the Boeing Chinook helicopter in 1981. July 1983 saw the first Lockheed TriStar tanker/transport aircraft and the first Vickers VC10 K2 tankers enter service. In the following year the McDonnell Douglas Phantom

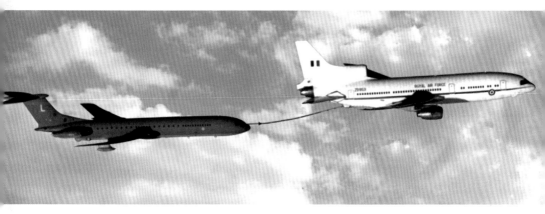

F3 fighter was introduced to provide
full-time cover on the Falklands and in
1986 a smaller transport aircraft, the BAe
146, entered service with The Queens
Flight. Developments of the Harrier
and Tornado – the GR5 and F3 – were
introduced in 1987, followed by the
Short Tucano trainer in 1989.

The 1990s saw the Harrier GR7
arrive in 1990 followed the next year
by the Boeing Sentry AEW1. Another
trainer, the Slingsby Firefly, entered
service in 1996 and the Bell Griffin
HT1 helicopter trainer was introduced
in 1997. The Lockheed Hercules C4
rounded off the decade in 1999.

The Falklands War

The invasion of the Falkland Islands by
the forces of Argentina on 2 April 1982
triggered Operation Corporate. The RAF
was called upon immediately and sent
four Hercules transport aircraft to RAF
Gibraltar to form part of a personnel
and equipment supply chain between
Britain and the forward operating base at
Wideawake Air base on Ascension Island
in the South Atlantic. A day later a VC10
of No 10 Squadron from RAF Brize
Norton in Oxfordshire was despatched
to Montevideo in Uruguay to collect
the British Governor of the Falkland
Islands and a party of Royal Marines

◀ Lockheed
Tristar delivers
fuel to a Vickers
VC10.

◀ Phantom
refuelling from a
Hercules tanker.

captured by Argentine forces during the invasion of the islands they referred to as 'Las Malvinas'. The VC10s continued to operate between Montevideo and the UK and flew many casualties from the conflict back to Britain.

Two Nimrod MR1 aircraft from No 42 Squadron left RAF St. Mawgan in Cornwall for Ascension Island, where they engaged in long-range patrols in support of the British Task Force, supplemented by Nimrod MR2s from Nos 120, 201 and 206 Squadrons. On 18 April five Victor K2 tankers arrived at Wideawake from where they were engaged initially in maritime radar reconnaissance flights over the South Atlantic around the islands of South Georgia and the Falklands. On one such mission a radar patrol by a Victor covered some 150,000 square miles of ocean in 14 hours and 45 minutes. Just three days later the RAF lost two Wessex helicopters in bad weather while attempting to evacuate Special Air Service (SAS) troops from South Georgia.

Following the imposition by Britain of a 200-mile radius 'no-fly' zone around the Falklands, it became apparent that the Task Force was about to take the first punitive action against the occupying forces. In preparation, the first Vulcan B2 bombers arrived at Ascension Island on 29 April. The first offensive sortie of the campaign took place over the two days of 30 April and 1 May. In the longest-range bombing sortie the RAF had undertaken, the Black Buck 1 mission, flown by a Vulcan B2 and supported by 18 Victor K2 tanker sorties, dropped twenty-one 1,000lb bombs across the runway at Port Stanley. The Vulcan returned safely to the Ascension Island base after a flight time of 15 hours and 45 minutes. Fleet Air Arm Sea Harriers followed this up with a further attack on the airstrip at Goose Green.

Two days later the second Vulcan attack mission, Black Buck 2, dropped a further twenty-one 1,000lb bombs on the Port Stanley airfield. Although later reconnaissance showed that these had landed close to the runway, the damage caused by the previous attack was still un-repaired. Black Buck 3 and 4 missions were flown on 31 May and 4 June, in which Shrike anti-radar missiles were launched against Argentine Skyguard installations on the Falklands. During Black Buck 4, the Vulcan sustained damage to its refuelling probe

and diverted to Rio de Janeiro in Brazil, where it was impounded until 10 June. Black Buck 5, the final mission, was made on 12 June with 1,000lb bombs directed against concentrations of Argentine troops near Port Stanley.

Although it was subsequently shown that the Black Buck operations had little direct military effect on the outcome of the Falklands War, there were several indirect benefits. As well as providing a 'morale boosting' effect on the British population of the Falklands, there was an opposite effect on the morale of the Argentine military forces of occupation. The theatre of operations also highlighted the need for the provision of an in-flight refuelling capability in those

▲ Westland Wessex HC2 of No. 72 Squadron.

◀ Nimrod receiving fuel from a Victor tanker.

RAF combat and transport aircraft that were, as yet, not fitted with the necessary systems. The provision and installation of such equipment at very short notice tested the ingenuity of both the British aircraft industry and the engineering staff of the RAF.

On 7 May the first Nimrod fitted with an in-flight refuelling probe was deployed to Wideawake Air Base and subsequently became the first Nimrod to carry out an extended anti-submarine patrol with in-flight refuelling. The next day a Westland Sea King HAR3 was flown to Ascension Island in an ex-RAF Belfast transport aircraft operated by the civil company Heavylift to provide both Search and Rescue (SAR) cover and local transportation around the island. A combined force of 20 Harriers and Sea Harriers also arrived at Ascension Island that day after a non-stop flight of around nine hours with in-flight refuelling. A further six RAF Harrier GR3s arrived in the South Atlantic by sea aboard the container ship *Atlantic Conveyor*, from where they flew to join the aircraft carrier HMS *Hermes*.

On 19 May the RAF's only fatality of the campaign occurred in a flying accident. Flight Lieutenant G W Hawkins, a Forward Air Controller, lost his life when the Sea King helicopter in which he was a passenger crashed into the sea after a suspected bird strike. Twenty of the twenty-nine personnel on board lost their lives.

Three Harrier GR3s undertook a successful cluster bomb raid against a fuel dump at Fox Bay in West Falkland on 20 May, with no RAF casualties. To protect the Wideawake base against attack by the Argentine Air Force, three McDonnell Douglas Phantom FGR2 aircraft were deployed to Ascension Island by 26 May for Quick Reaction Alert (QRA) defence duties, and remained there until late in July.

On 21 May, following SAS intelligence reports that Argentine helicopters had been hidden in a hollow between Mount Kent and Mount Estancia, two Harrier GR3s from HMS *Hermes* set off at first light. One of the helicopters, a Bell UH-1D Huey, was already airborne at the time of the

attack and made good its escape. The remaining two Pumas and a Chinook were hit by 30mm cannon rounds from the Harriers and caught fire. One of the Harriers was hit by three bullets from ground fire, but returned safely to HMS *Hermes*. On the same day the RAF lost its first Harrier when a GR3 of No 1 Squadron was shot down, probably by a surface-to-air missile. Its pilot, Flight Lieutenant Glover, ejected successfully but was injured and subsequently taken prisoner. After treatment at Comodoro Rivadavia on the Argentine mainland, he was eventually repatriated after all hostilities had ceased.

One of the blackest days of the operation for British forces was 25 May 1982, which saw the loss of two vessels – HMS *Coventry* and the *Atlantic Conveyor*. Apart from the tragic loss of life involved, the latter's cargo included three RAF Chinook helicopters and a further six RN helicopters.

The second Harrier GR3 lost in the conflict was shot down by radar-controlled anti-aircraft gunfire near Goose Green on 27 May. Its pilot, Squadron Leader Bob Iveson, ejected safely, hid away and was later rescued

◀ HMS
Coventry.

WAR AND THE PEACE DIVIDEND

◀ Tornado GR1.

by helicopter. Three days later another Harrier GR3 was hit by ground fire near Port Stanley. The resulting damage caused a fuel shortage that prevented the aircraft from returning to HMS *Hermes*; the pilot, Squadron Leader Pook, ejected safely into the sea and was rescued. RAF pilots were also active in the Sea Harrier force. One of these, Flight Lieutenant D Morgan, became the top scoring British pilot of the campaign, shooting down four Argentinean aircraft, an achievement for which he was awarded the Distinguished Service Cross.

During the Falklands War RAF transport aircraft played a significant role in the supply chain to both Ascension Island and onward to the occupied territory. Within the Falklands one of the most important contributions to the British effort was afforded by the lone surviving Chinook helicopter that operated initially without spares or tools, as these had gone down with the *Atlantic Conveyor*.

Major contributions were made by the VC10s and Hercules aircraft that ferried men and equipment between the UK, Ascension Island and the Falklands. Some of the Hercules had been hurriedly modified with internal long-range fuel tanks and fitted with in-flight refuelling probes to extend their range. Others were converted to provide tanker facilities via a refuelling hose and drogue system fitted through the modified cargo bay door. Although too late for use in the conflict, these tankers provided valuable facilities for garrison defence fighters in the post-war period following the surrender of Argentine troops on 14 June 1982.

Desert Shield And Desert Storm

Iraqi forces invaded and occupied Kuwait on 2 August 1990 and four days later King Fahd of Saudi Arabia requested military support from governments that were friendly towards his country. Operation Granby commenced almost immediately. By 11 August British combat aircraft were arriving in the Gulf area in the form of 12 Tornado F3 air defence fighters that fortuitously had been attending an Armament Practice Camp in Cyprus. Two days later 12 Jaguar GR1A ground attack aircraft arrived in Oman prior to being re-deployed one month later to Bahrain.

The Saudi Arabian airfield at Dhahran soon began to fill with RAF personnel and equipment brought by RAF Hercules and TriStar transports.

The air base at Seeb in Oman saw the arrival of two VC10 tankers and three Nimrod MR2 aircraft. The build-up continued with the arrival at Muharraq of a Tornado GR1 detachment from Germany at the end of August. At the beginning of November a detachment of Hercules was established at King Khalid International Airport in Riyadh, Saudi Arabia and shortly before Christmas the first four of eight Victor tankers arrived in Muharraq, the remainder arriving early in January. Further deployments of Tornado GR1s arrived at Tabuk and Dhahran by the first week in January 1991 and RAF assets in the area were further boosted by the arrival of a reconnaissance detachment of six Tornado GR1As at Dhahran on 14 January.

Operation Desert Storm began on 16-17 January 1991 with an air assault on Iraqi airfields and key military installations. The first RAF attacks on Iraqi airfields were carried out using a variety of ordnance, including 1,000lb bombs and Hunting JP233 airfield denial munitions. The first RAF loss occurred when a Tornado was shot down by a surface-to-air missile after a low-altitude bombing attack on Ar Rumaylah air base in Southern Iraq; its crew ejected and were taken prisoner. They were beaten, tortured and later paraded on television by their captors, who showed no respect for the Geneva Convention regarding the treatment of prisoners of war. Another Tornado was shot down on 18 January with the loss of both of its crew. In total, six Tornado GR1s were lost in the campaign; of the twelve aircrew, five lost their lives.

With continuing attacks on Iraqi Scud missile sites and other critical targets, the RAF Tornadoes, Jaguars and Buccaneers made valuable contributions to the war effort, with support from other RAF resources including the medical, logistics, airfield defence and communications specialisations. Aerial offensive sorties continued as preparations for the ground offensive were under way. The Allies successfully cut all the main supply routes to the beleaguered Iraqi ground troops, including bridges, rail links and highways. The war to regain Kuwait was effectively won after a four-day ground assault, and hostilities officially ceased on 29 February 1991.

The Balkans

On 31 March 1993 RAF assets were deployed as part of a NATO force in Operation Deny Flight that was set up to police a 'no-fly' zone over Bosnia. This involved RAF Tornado F3s, Boeing Sentry AEW1s and Jaguars, supported by VC10 tankers. RAF Hercules provided an airlift of humanitarian aid and supplies into the area and also took part in the evacuation of casualties from Sarajevo to Britain for specialised medical treatment.

Due to the ongoing and escalating problems in the area, the NATO forces commenced Operation Deliberate Force on 30 August 1995 in an effort to protect the population of the Sarajevo area. In the following two weeks RAF aircraft flew 268 sorties in which they dropped thirty-two 1,000lb bombs and forty-eight laser-guided bombs against twenty-two targets. In December 1995 three RAF Chinook helicopters formed part of the Support Helicopter Force based at Split in Croatia, from where they assisted a multi-national force to implement the Dayton Peace Accord.

The RAF continued its involvement in the former Yugoslavia for the

◄ No. 13 Squadron Tornado GR4A.

next three years. In March 1999, following the breakdown in talks, NATO forces took part in Operation Allied Force to force the withdrawal of Serbian troops from Kosovo. The NATO strategy was to carry out an intensive and systematic bombing campaign against Serbian forces in Kosovo and also against key targets within Serbia itself. The RAF was involved in Operation Allied Force from the outset. On 24 March 1999, the first night of the operation, six BAe Harrier GR7 aircraft, supported by Lockheed TriStar tankers and Boeing Sentry Airborne Early Warning

aircraft, participated in an attack on an ammunition store in Serbia. The attack was aborted due to smoke over the objective that prevented the laser-guided bombs from locking onto their designated targets.

On 4 and 5 April 1999 six Tornado GR1s from RAF Bruggen in Germany, supported by VC10 tankers, attacked bridges and tunnels on the Serbian supply routes into Kosovo. One month later 12 Tornado GR1s were deployed to the French Air Force base at Solenzara in Corsica, but shortly after carrying out their first offensive operation NATO suspended air operations against Serbian forces, which began to withdraw. RAF helicopters, including six Pumas and eight Chinooks, took part in Operation Agricola wherein British troops were deployed into Kosovo in the largest support helicopter deployment since Operation Granby in the 1990 Gulf War. By the third week in June 1999, Serbian troops had completed their withdrawal and a NATO peacekeeping force was in place in Kosovo.

Desert Fox And The No-Fly Zones

Operation Desert Fox was intended to both degrade the infrastructure associated with Iraq's ability to manufacture and deploy 'weapons of mass destruction' and reduce the Iraqi military capability for aggression against its neighbouring states, including Israel. Following air-strikes and cruise missile attacks by United States forces against targets in Iraq on 16 and 17 December 1998, RAF Tornado GR1s left their base in Kuwait to attack military targets near Basra.

During the first two months of 1999 RAF Tornadoes flew many sorties against military installations, including Iraqi ground-radar sites that were known to be tracking British and

▲ Harrier GR7.

American aircraft policing the 'No-Fly' zone in southern Iraq. In many cases the Paveway laser-guided bomb was used against these targets, more than 60 being dropped in the month of January.

The Strategic Defence Review

Once again the RAF together with the Army and Royal Navy faced the imposed task of re-organisation in response to policy changes that were included in the 1997 Strategic Defence Review (SDR). One of its features was the combination and use of assets to support all three services, for example the formation of Joint Force Harrier,

▲ Tornado GR4A.

although the Eurofighter project was to continue. There was also an acknowledged requirement for a Tornado GR4 replacement. The procurement of armaments, such as the Storm Shadow stand-off attack missile that entered service in 2002 and the Brimstone anti-armour missile that came into service in 2004, improved the RAF's strike capability. Until such time as the Meteor entered service, the Typhoon would be armed with the advanced medium range air-to-air missile (Amraam).

The accelerated retirement of the we177 tactical nuclear weapon occurred on 31 march 1998, when the last 'bucket of instant sunshine' was withdrawn from RAF service. In the aftermath of the terrorist attacks on New York and Washington on 11 September 2001 (9/11), a further chapter of the strategic defence review was announced. These plans included, amongst others, the placing of RAF air defence assets on quick reaction alert (QRA) standby in order to counter any potential terrorist aerial attack on the UK, including the use of hijacked civilian aircraft.

Joint Helicopter Command, Joint Rapid Reaction Force and Joint Nuclear Biological Chemical Regiment.

'Mobility' was one of the keywords of the SDR. The review recognised the requirement for a strategic transport force, with the RAF requirement being filled in the short term by the lease of four Boeing C-17 Globemaster aircraft that were later purchased outright.

The RAF was once again required to undergo a further 'downsizing'. Its 'fast jet' force was to be reduced by two squadrons – around 36 aircraft –

Into The Future

The Raf In
The 21st Century

In 2007 a single HQ Air Command was formed from the merger of Personnel and Training Command and Strike Command in order to meet the needs of the modern RAF. Tactical helicopter units are under the control of the multi-service Joint Helicopter Command.

Under the new structure the trend towards the civilianisation of support services has continued. Specific operational roles are delegated to three 'groups'. No 1 Group is known as the Air Combat Group, and operates all fast jet combat aircraft. No 2 Group, the Air Combat Support Group, operates logistic support transport aircraft, air-to-air refuelling tankers, the maritime patrol and reconnaissance aircraft, the Search and Rescue (SAR) helicopters, the Mountain Rescue Service, and all Airborne Early Warning (AEW) aircraft and ground based air defence radar installations throughout the UK. The Group also has Intelligence,

Surveillance, Target Acquisition and Reconnaissance (ISTAR) and Force Protection (FP) functions.

A third group, No 22 (Training) Group, exists to recruit and train RAF personnel and provide trained specialists to the RAF and the other two Services. The group also operated the RAF Aerobatic Team, better known as the Red Arrows.

New Aircraft For The New Millennium

The new millennium saw the delivery in February 2000 of the first Panavia Tornado GR4. With its updated and advanced avionics and weapon systems, the Tornado GR4 is expected to remain in service with the RAF until 2025. The first of the new Lockheed Hercules C130J variant, with its reduced flight deck crew of two, also became operational that year.

Early in March 2001 the first Merlin HC3 helicopter was delivered, while in

INTO THE FUTURE

▲ C-17 Globemaster III transport during stopover in the Gulf area, 2003.

aircraft was assembled, while detailed development and testing was carried out. Formal activation of a Typhoon Squadron occurred on 1 July 2005, and the aircraft was declared combat ready in July 2008. The Typhoon is a multi-role combat aircraft, capable of being deployed in the full spectrum of operations, from air policing to peace support to high intensity conflict. In May 2007 the SEPECAT Jaguar was taken out of service as the Typhoon became more prevalent.

The Raytheon Sentinel R1 came into service in December 2008 and is fitted with Airborne Stand-Off Radar (ASTOR) to provide a long-range, battlefield-intelligence, target-imaging and tracking radar. In 2009 the RAF received the first of 28 BAE Hawk Mk 128 Advanced Jet Trainer (AJT) aircraft, known within the RAF as the Hawk T2. However, the aircraft has been put in storage pending the development of a new flying training course. The aircraft has a fully digital cockpit coupled with airborne simulation systems and will be used to train pilots to fly the new-generation digital-cockpit fighter aircraft such as the Eurofighter Typhoon and the

May the first Boeing C17 Globemaster III strategic transport aircraft formally entered RAF service.

During the Fire Brigade Union's industrial dispute in 2002, over 3,000 RAF personnel provided fire-fighting cover for the UK in Operation Fresco. The Advanced Short-Range Air-to-Air missile (ASRAAM) also entered RAF service that year.

The Bell Griffin HAR2 helicopter entered service in January 2003, replacing the venerable Westland Wessex. That year deliveries of the Eurofighter Typhoon began to a squadron based at the BAE aerodrome alongside the factory in which the

▲ First prototype
of the Raytheon
Sentinel R1
Airborne
Stand-off Radar
(ASTOR) aircraft.

F-35 Joint Combat Aircraft. It will also be capable of carrying out ground attack and air defence roles.

Meanwhile, the fleet of Nimrod MR2s was withdrawn from service in March 2010 – a year earlier than originally planned – as part of a range of defence cuts.

Iraqi Freedom

The air policing operations in the 'No-Fly' zones of Iraq were stood down in March 2003 in preparation for the commencement of Operation Telic, the British part of the US-led Operation Iraq Freedom. Operation Telic required the movement of a vast number of British troops, their equipment and support services. Almost one-third of the RAF's available strength in manpower was committed, along with a large contribution to the strike, reconnaissance and airborne refuelling requirements of the coalition forces. The RAF flew over 2,500 sorties against ground targets and lost 22 RAF personnel in the course of Operation Telic.

Many new types of equipment were used in action for the first time including the Raptor reconnaissance pod and the Alarm 2 anti-radiation missile for the Tornado GR4, and another new reconnaissance pod for the Harrier GR7. The Tornado also carried Storm Shadow, a long-range stand-off weapon, and the Enhanced Paveway precision strike

▲ Chinook
helicopter.

weapon. The Harrier GR7 received the
proven Raytheon Maverick precision all-
weather strike weapon.

Major combat operations by
coalition forces ceased on 1 May
2003 and the RAF began working
towards reconstruction, with the
development of Basra Airfield into
Basra International Airport.

After operating in and over Iraq for
almost 19 years – one of the longest
deployments in RAF history – the
British military mission in Iraq officially
came to a close on 30 April 2009 and
the RAF ensign was lowered at Basra

airport in May. A small number of
personnel and equipment remain in and
around Iraq to assist the Foreign and
Commonwealth Office and provide air
transport in and out of Iraq.

Afghanistan

Following the terrorist attacks on the
United States on September 11 2001, since
referred to as 9/11, Britain joined with
the United States in military operations
against the terrorist training camps of Al
Qaeda and the Taliban air defence targets
in Afghanistan. These missions commenced
on 7 October 2001 with bombing attacks

by both United States and RAF aircraft. As well as carrying out attacks against terrorist targets, the civilian population was targeted in humanitarian operations involving an airlift of food and medical supplies. Following the initial operations, RAF aircraft played a major part in re-supply operations in support of ground forces and also provided tankers for air-to-air refuelling of patrolling fighters and reconnaissance aircraft.

In a deployment timed to assist in the maintenance of order during the presidential elections in October 2004, six Harrier GR7 aircraft were based in Kandahar under Coalition control to provide close air-support and reconnaissance capability.

In a tragic accident, an RAF Nimrod MR2 patrol aircraft crashed near Kandahar on 2 September 2006, killing all 14 service members aboard.

Harriers remained in Afghanistan until June 2009, when Tornado GR4s replaced the eight Harrier GR7s and GR9s which had flown for more than 22,000 hours on over 8,500 sorties in the five years they were there.

Current RAF support in Afghanistan comprises about 950 RAF personnel.

The Tornado GR4s now provide tactical reconnaissance and close air support, and in-theatre airlift is provided by C130s and supplemented by the HS125 and BAe 146. TriStars provide air refuelling support for coalition aircraft and with C17 aircraft move personnel and material into and out of the region. Chinook helicopters provide key to tactical mobility for land forces. Kandahar airfield is protected by the RAF Regiment and RAF Police, and 1 Air Control Centre provides airspace management in Helmand province.

Afghanistan remains the MoD's top priority.

▲ Members of No. 1 Squadron, Royal Air Force Regiment patrolling the perimeter of Basra air base in southern Iraq, 2005.

▲ Lockheed Martin F-35 Joint Strike Fighter/Joint Combat Aircraft. Flags of the nine customer countries are displayed on the tail fin.

The Raf Of The Future

The government's Strategic Defence and Security Review published in October 2010 sets out how the Armed Forces will be reshaped to tackle emerging and future threats.

The RAF's capabilities that will be taking us into the future include a modernised multi-role Typhoon fleet and the Joint Strike Fighter (JSF) to provide combat intelligence, surveillance, target acquisition and reconnaissance

(ISTAR) capabilities.

In addition, E-3D Sentry AWACS (Airborne Warning and Control System) provide airborne command, control and surveillance; Rivet Joint signals intelligence aircraft allow for independent strategic intelligence gathering; and a range of remotely piloted air systems are also available.

The air transport fleet will be upgraded with the addition of the Airbus A400M transport aircraft and the Airbus A330 future strategic tanker and transport aircraft to operate alongside the C17 fleet. These aircraft will enable rapid deployment, support and recovery of UK forces and their equipment anywhere in the world, and provide airborne refuelling to maximise the range and endurance of other aircraft.

The support helicopter capability (both RAF and Royal Navy) will continue to provide battlefield mobility from land and sea, based on Chinook and Merlin helicopters able to move personnel and equipment rapidly over considerable distances.

However, in order to meet this new structure the RAF will lose around 5,000 personnel to bring it to about 33,000 by

▲ Eurofighter
Typhoon T1s.

2015, and with an assumed requirement of about 31,500 by 2020; in addition it will lose 25-30 per cent of its civilian staff.

The C130 Hercules transport fleet will be withdrawn ten years earlier than planned, the Sentinel surveillance aircraft will be withdrawn once it is no longer required to support operations in Afghanistan; the Harrier was removed from service in December 2010 and the VC10 and the three variants of TriStar aircraft will be withdrawn from 2013. The construction of the Nimrod MRA4 reconnaissance plane has been terminated and the part-built fleet destroyed.

Whatever the future holds, the RAF is justifiably proud of a history that spans a period of less than a hundred years. From the era of the balloon and kite to the latest advances in technology, the RAF has evolved to face each new challenge and will adapt to those ahead. There will always be those who, 'Through Struggles to the Stars', will overcome adversity and add to its achievements, while upholding the values and traditions of their predecessors.

To download our latest catalogue and to view
the full range of books and DVDs visit:

www.G2ent.co.uk